NAVIGATING
THE GOLDEN COMPASS

OTHER TITLES IN THE SMART POP SERIES

Taking the Red Pill
Science, Philosophy and Religion in The Matrix

Seven Seasons of Buffy
Science Fiction and Fantasy Writers Discuss Their Favorite Television Show

Five Seasons of Angel
Science Fiction and Fantasy Writers Discuss Their Favorite Vampire

Stepping Through the Stargate
Science, Archaeology and the Military in Stargate SG-1

What Would Sipowicz Do?
Race, Rights and Redemption in NYPD Blue

The Anthology at the End of the Universe
Leading Science Fiction Authors
on Douglas Adams' Hitchhiker's Guide to the Galaxy

Finding Serenity
Anti-heroes, Lost Shepherds and Space Hookers in Joss Whedon's Firefly

The War of the Worlds
Fresh Perspectives on the H. G. Wells Classic

Alias Assumed
Sex, Lies and SD-6

NAVIGATING THE GOLDEN COMPASS

RELIGION, SCIENCE
AND DÆMONOLOGY IN
HIS DARK MATERIALS

EDITED BY

GLENN YEFFETH

BENBELLA BOOKS, INC.
Dallas, Texas

BenBella Books, Inc.
6440 N. Central Expressway, Suite 617
Dallas, TX 75206
www.benbellabooks.com
Send feedback to feedback@benbellabooks.com

PUBLISHER: Glenn Yeffeth
EDITOR: Shanna Caughey
ASSOCIATE EDITOR: Leah Wilson
DIRECTOR OF MARKETING/PR: Laura Watkins

Printed in the United States of America
10 9 8 7 6 5 4 3 2 1

Library of Congress Cataloging-in-Publication Data
Navigating The golden compass : religion, science, and daemonology in His dark materials / edited by Glenn Yeffeth.
p. cm.
ISBN 1-932100-52-0
1. Pullman, Philip, 1946- His dark materials. 2. Young adult fiction, English--History and criticism. 3. Fantasy fiction, English—History and criticism. 4. Demonology in literature. 5. Religion in literature. 6. Science in literature. I. Yeffeth, Glenn, 1961–

PR6066.U44H56 2005
823'.914—dc22

2005012755

Cover design by Todd Michael Bushman
Text design and composition by John Reinhardt Book Design

Distributed by Independent Publishers Group
To order call (800) 888-4741
www.ipgbook.com

For special sales contact Laura Watkins at laura@benbellabooks.com

Contents

Dust & Dæmons

This piece first appeared in *The New York Review of Books* in 2004.

1.

Pity those—adventurers, adolescents, authors of young adult fiction— who make their way in the borderland between worlds. It is at worst an invisible and at best an inhospitable place. Build your literary house on the borderlands, as the English writer Philip Pullman has done, and you may find that your work is recommended by booksellers, as a stop-gap between installments of Harry Potter, to children who cannot (one hopes) fully appreciate it, and to adults, disdainful or baffled, who "don't read fantasy." Yet all mystery resides there, in the margins, between life and death, childhood and adulthood, Newtonian and quantum, "serious" and "genre" literature. And it is from the confrontation with mystery that the truest stories have always drawn their power.

Like a house on the borderlands, epic fantasy is haunted: by a sense of lost purity and grandeur, deep wisdom that has been forgotten, Arcadia spoilt, the debased or diminished stature of modern humankind; by a sense that the world, to borrow a term from John Clute, the Canadian-born British critic of fantasy and science fiction, has "thinned." This sense of thinning—of there having passed a Golden Age, a Dreamtime, when animals spoke, magic worked, children honored their parents, and fish leapt filleted into the skillet—has haunted the telling of stories from the beginning. The words "Once upon a time" are in part a kind of magic formula for invoking the ache of this primordial nostalgia.

But serious literature, so called, regularly traffics in the same wistful stuff. One encounters the unassuageable ache of the imagined past, for example, at a more or less implicit level, in American writers from Cooper and Hawthorne through Faulkner and Chandler, right down to Steven Millhauser and Jonathan Franzen. Epic fantasy distills and abstracts the idea of thinning—*maps* it, so to speak; but at its best the genre is no less serious or literary than any other. Yet epic fantasies, whether explicitly written for children or not, tend to get sequestered in their own section of the bookstore or library, clearly labeled to protect the unsuspecting reader of naturalistic fiction from making an awkward mistake. Thus do we consign to the borderlands our most audacious retellings of what is arguably one of the two or three primal human stories: the narrative of Innocence, Experience, and, straddling the margin between them, the Fall.

Any list of the great British works of epic fantasy must begin with *Paradise Lost*, with its dark lord, cursed tree, invented cosmology and ringing battle scenes, its armored angelic cavalries shattered by demonic engines of war. But most typical works of contemporary epic fantasy have (consciously at least) followed Tolkien's model rather than Milton's, dressing in Norse armor and Celtic shadow the ache of Innocence Lost, and then, crucially, figuring it *as a landscape*, a broken fairyland where brazen experience has replaced the golden days of innocence; where, as in the Chronicles of Narnia, it is "always winter and never Christmas."

A recent exception to the Tolkienesque trend is Pullman's series of three novels, *The Golden Compass*, *The Subtle Knife*, and *The Amber Spyglass* (with a promised fourth, *The Book of Dust*), which reshuffle, reinterpret, and draw from Milton's epic both a portion of their strength and their collective title: His Dark Materials. Pullman, who was a student at Oxford in the 1960s, has just served up a new volume, a kind of tasty sherbet course in the ongoing banquet, entitled *Lyra's Oxford*.

There are broken lands in His Dark Materials—there are entire broken universes, in fact, whose vital stuff is leaking from them into the Miltonic abyss at a frightening rate. But the central figuring of Innocence and the Fall Pullman accomplishes neither through the traditional mapping of a landscape nor, as in Jack Vance's classic *The Dying Earth*,[1] through

---

[1] Originally published in 1950 in a cheap paperback edition by the comic-book publisher Hillman Periodicals; currently available, with its three sequels, in the omnibus *Tales of the Dying Earth* (Tor Books, 2000).

melancholy reiteration of the depleted catalog of a once-vast library of magical texts and spells. Instead, Pullman has looked around at this broken universe of ours, in its naturalistic tatters, and has indicated, like Satan pointing to the place on which Pandimonium will rise, the site of our truest contemporary narratives of the Fall: in the lives, in the bodies and souls, of our children.

2.

Lyra Belacqua is a girl of ten or eleven when *The Golden Compass*, the first volume of the series, begins. Her parentage, in the traditional manner, is uncertain, at least to her. She is headstrong, cheerful, forthright, loyal, and articulate, rather in the Dorothy Gale style of female fantasy heroines. She is also an uncouth, intractable, manipulative liar, and occasionally stupid. The first time we encounter her, she is engaged in an act of inadvisable disobedience—trespassing in the Retiring Room at Jordan College, Oxford, which is strictly off-limits to all but Scholars—one whose consequences, which she imagines as no worse than chastisement, will include but not be limited to wide-scale ecological disaster and the death of her best friend. She has, in other words, a complexity of character, and a tragic weakness unusual for a work of children's literature, and in fact the question of whether or not His Dark Materials is meant or even suitable for young readers not only remains open but grows ever more difficult to answer as the series progresses. This indeterminacy of readership—the way Pullman's story pulses fitfully between the poles of adult and children's fiction, illuminating by weird flashes that vague middle zone known in the librarian trade as YA—is, as I have already suggested, itself a figuring- or working-out of the fundamental plot of His Dark Materials, which turns, and turns again, on the question of what becomes of us, of our bodies and our souls, as we enter the borderland of adolescence.

Lyra lives in a room at Jordan College, Oxford, where she has led a half-feral, largely pleasurable life as the seditious, indifferently educated ward of the college, looked after by a gruff old housekeeper and a faculty of male scholars who have no idea what to make of or do with her. Her childhood, an unbroken series of small adventures, hair-raising exploits, and minor wars among the local tribes of Oxford's children, is evoked by Pullman in the first book's opening chapters with verve, humor, and the special poignance of his foreknowledge, and our strong suspicion, that it is Lyra's childhood—and indeed Childhood itself—that will prove to be the irrecoverable paradise, the Dreamtime, of his story.

There is, of course, no Jordan among the colleges of Oxford University. Lyra's Oxford exists in a different universe, one in which, as in our own, it is a primary center of learning and scholarship for England, Europe, and the world, has deep ecclesiastical roots, and sits astride the Thames River, on a bend known locally as the Isis. But in Lyra's world, though it strongly resembles our own in many ways—including possessing what appears to be an identical geography—evolution and history have taken different bends. Here, during the Reformation, the Holy See was transferred from Rome to Geneva; at some point John Calvin became pope. Somehow this, and a number of other premises, most of which Pullman leaves unstated, form a syllogism whose conclusion is a world united under the rule of a powerfully repressive Church Triumphant that is itself fatally divided among warring factions of bishops and prelates banded into orders whose names are at once bland, grand, and horrible: the Consistorial Court of Discipline, the General Oblation Board (charged with preparing oblations, or offerings, whose nature is at first a source of considerable mystery). What we know as science, in particular, physics, is viewed in Lyra's world as a subject fit for philosophers and above all for theologians—the study of fundamental particles is known there as *experimental theology*. Its discoveries are subject to ultimate review by the Church, and painful is the reward awaiting those, like a certain Russian Dr. Rusakov, who posit the existence of phenomena that violate Church teaching.

Lyra's world, with its shuffled deck of underlying premises, is technologically accomplished in ways that equal and even exceed our own—helped in this regard by its willingness to view as controllable natural phenomena what our world would call magic—and in other ways strangely retarded or perverse. Electric power is widely in use, though it is known as "anbaric power" (the terms are etymologically akin, deriving from the Greek and Arabic words for amber), produced by great river-spanning dynamos and "atom-craft" plants, but guns have no ascendancy, refrigeration and the science of food preservation appear to be unknown, and computers and automobiles are little in evidence. Instead travel proceeds on foot, by boat, or by that colophon of alternate-world fiction from *Ada* to *The League of Extraordinary Gentlemen*, the grand zeppelin liner. But for all its neo-Edwardian style, Lyra's Oxfordshire appears largely to remain sunk in the Middle Ages—agrarian, semi-feudal, reckoning its calendar by harvest and fair and by the seasonal comings and goings of a small, fierce nation of people known as gyptians, led by their king John Faa, whose name appears, in our world, in a well-known fifteenth-century English ballad about a gypsy king.

While Pullman alludes to Nabokov (one of the characters in *The Subtle Knife* voyages to Nova Zembla), his paired Oxfords stand in a very different relation from that of *Ada*'s Terra and Antiterra, which reflect and comment only upon each other, locked in a transdimensional self-regard which in turn mirrors that of the vain Van Veen. Instead, Pullman has consciously and overtly founded the structure of his fictional universe on the widely if not universally accepted "many-worlds hypothesis," derived from quantum physics—in His Dark Materials there will eventually turn out to be (rather conservatively) "millions" of such worlds, though in the end Pullman has only guided us through half a dozen of them.[2] Lyra's and ours are only two among the infinite number of possible Oxfords, all of which, according to the hypothesis at its most extreme, exist.

Pullman's use of such avant-garde scientific notions as the multiverse and dark matter (more on that later) might incline one to slap the label of "science fiction" onto his work along with "epic fantasy," "YA," and "alternate-world fiction"; but the quantum physics in His Dark Materials is mostly employed as a rationale for the standard world-hopping that heroes and heroines of fantasy have been engaging in from *Gilgamesh* onward. More interesting is Pullman's understanding of the metaphoric power of the many-worlds theory. An endlessly ramifying series of possibility-worlds, diverging and diverging again with each alteration in state, each tiny choice made, each selection of B over A: this may or may not be physics, but it is indisputably storytelling. And Pullman, as it turns out, is an unabashed concocter of stories, with a deep, pulpy fondness for plot. He is also, in the great tradition of unabashed concocters of stories, a highly self-conscious storyteller. By the end of *The Amber Spyglass*, one has come to see Pullman's world-calving imagination, to see Imagination itself, as the ordering principle, if not of the universe itself, then of our ability to comprehend, to wander, and above all to love it.

---

[2] Pullman avoids use of the term "multiverse," arguably coined by the greatest writer of post-Tolkien British fantasy, Michael Moorcock, to whose work Pullman's is clearly indebted.

3.

However far the narrative may wander, the action of His Dark Materials centers tightly, even obsessively, on the interrelation of two of Pullman's many felicitous inventions: dæmons and Dust.

The goddess of writers was smiling upon Philip Pullman on the day he came up with the idea for dæmons. These are, in Lyra's world, the inseparable life companions of every human being. Dæmons take the shapes of animals, but they have reason and the power of speech. Lyra's is named Pantalaimon—she calls him Pan—and at first we take him to be her animal familiar, but we soon learn that he is in fact the equivalent of what is known in our world as the soul. The bond between human and dæmon is fundamental, essential, empathic, and at times telepathic. When a dæmon's human being dies, its own life ends; the dæmon winks out of existence, snuffed like a candle flame. Pan, like all children's dæmons, has not yet "settled"—that is, he can take on, at will, the shape of any animal he wishes, a power he will retain until Lyra reaches puberty. When Pan is frightened or anxious to conceal himself, he is a moth, or a mouse; when he wishes to intimidate or to repel attack he becomes a snarling wildcat; when Lyra is feeling lonely or cold he becomes a soft, warm ermine and drapes himself tenderly around her neck.

As the story unfolds, new wrinkles and refinements in the relationship between human and dæmon keep occurring to Pullman, and he reports them to us at once with the palpable storyteller's excitement that animates (and at times undermines) the entire series: while people generally have dæmons of the opposite gender to their own, some rare oddballs have a same-sex dæmon; people tend to get the dæmons they deserve (schemers have snake dæmons, servants have dog dæmons); there is a painful limit to the distance by which a human and a dæmon can stand to be separated, except in the case of the witches of the North—those Lapland witches mentioned by Milton in Book II of *Paradise Lost?*—who undergo a fearsome initiation rite that enables them and their dæmons to travel separately. And so on. My eight-year-old daughter expressed what I imagine is a near-universal response of readers, young and old, to His Dark Materials (and probably the ultimate secret of the series' success): "I wonder what kind of dæmon I would have!"

When we meet them, Lyra and her dæmon are spying on hastily organized preparations for the return to Jordan College of the man she

believes to be her uncle, Lord Asriel, an explorer and inventor of formidable reputation. Pan has advised against this foray into the forbidden
Retiring Room, and he flutters anxiously on her shoulder, having taken
for the moment the fearful, flighty form of a moth. It is here, hidden in
a wardrobe full of scholar's gowns, that Lyra and we first encounter the
sparkling puzzle of Dust.

Lord Asriel has just returned from the North, where he led an expedition (lovingly outfitted by Pullman, like all the novels' several expeditions, with the full Shackletonian panoply of late-Victorian explorers'
gear) to observe the phenomena known, after the Church-burned her-
etic who first described them, as Rusakov particles, or Dust. All of the
novels' villains, demagogues, and amoral researchers, as well as a number of its finer, nobler characters—Pullman, true to his YA roots, has a
tendency to lay on the fine and the noble with a rather heavy spackling
knife—believe, or come to believe, that the continued existence of the
theocratic, Church-determined, hierarchical universe as they know it
depends on understanding the mysterious charged particles known in
our world as dark matter and in Lyra's as Dust. These invisible particles
seem to be connected in some way to the Aurora Borealis, and they have
the curious property (as Lord Asriel proceeds to demonstrate by means
of a photographic process of his own invention, with Lyra and Pan, concealed in the wardrobe, hanging on his every word) of being powerfully
attracted to adult human beings, settling on them like dander or snow,
while appearing to be completely uninterested, if particles can be said
to take interest (and they can!), in children.

Lord Asriel has returned from the North to hit up the College for
more funding, ostensibly so that he can continue his purely scientific
research into the puzzling nature of Dust. In reality he intends to follow
the trail of falling Dust out of Lyra's and her dæmon's world and into
another. He doesn't mention this, however, or that implementing his
plan of opening a breach through the boreal "thin patch" will require
the sacrifice of a child by means of a horrific brand of metaphysical vivi-
section known as "intercision."

Intercision is also the business of the General Oblation Board, an
arm of the Church that has recently begun a spectacular rise to power
under the direction of Mrs. Coulter, its lay chairman. Mrs. Coulter is,
until she receives an unfortunate first name (the far too British *Vogue*
"Marisa") and even more unfortunately a heart somewhere around the
second quarter of *The Amber Spyglass*, one of the great villains of re-

cent popular literature, right up there, in viciousness, strength, intelligence, and inexorableness, with *Lonesome Dove's* (unredeemed to the end) Blue Duck. Mrs. Coulter, beautiful, elegant, capable of simulating terrible charm and warmth, her natural mode a fittingly polar coldness, accompanied everywhere by her truly scary golden monkey dæmon, has the power, like all good *femmes fatales*, to cloud men's minds.

Under her spell, and frightened by the implications of Dust's evident attraction to experience in the Blakean sense, to Fallenness—believing that Dust may be the physical manifestation of Original Sin itself—the Church leadership has authorized Mrs. Coulter to lead a northern expedition of her own, one that will seek to determine whether Dust—Sin—can be forestalled, fended off, or eliminated entirely, by the intercision of a child before his or her dæmon has "settled." Naturally this course of research, carried on at a remote post in the Arctic, where Dust streams most plentifully, requires a steady supply of pre-adolescent subjects. Under Mrs. Coulter's orders, teams of child-snatchers—known semimythically among the local children as "Gobblers"—fan out across England, baiting their traps with sweets and kindness. When her best friend at the College, a servant's child named Roger, is stolen away by Mrs. Coulter's General Oblation Board, Lyra determines to set off for the North and save him.

The first volume of the sequence, *The Golden Compass*, is taken up with the competing schemes of Lord Asriel and Mrs. Coulter to understand and if possible control Dust, and with Lyra's quest to find Roger and at the same time to convey to Lord Asriel (funded again and back in the North) a marvelous contraption called an alethiometer. The alethiometer is Pullman's third great invention, after dæmons and Dust. A beautiful instrument of gold and crystal, engraved with an alphabet or tarot of conventional symbols and fitted with knurls and indicator needles, the alethiometer will answer any question put to it, though it will not predict the future. When it comes to reading the alethiometer, a skill that normally demands a lifetime of training and study, Lyra proves to be a natural.

Under the alethiometer's tutelage, and with the help of a troop of stout gyptians, Lyra makes her way north, learning, in the usual way of such journeys, even more about herself and her history than about the world she lives in, and discovering that there is a prophecy among the witches which she seems to be about to fulfill. Along the way she encounters an adventurer named Lee Scoresby, a Texan from New Denmark (her world's US), who comes equipped with a hot air balloon and a greasepaint-Texan manner that will be familiar to readers of Buchan and Conan Doyle; and the appealing Iorek Byrnison, who in spite of his Nordic name is a polar bear, or a kind of polar bear, polar bears having in Lyra's world evolved opposable thumbs (they are mighty smiths) and the power of speech. Interestingly it is Byrnison the bear and not Scoresby the Texan who plays the Lee Marvin role in this novel, rousing himself from an alcoholic miasma of failure—it all turns on a question of bear politics—through admiration of the gifted and fiery girl.

With the help of her companions, and following a number of hectic battles and one chilling scene of paternal anagnorisis or moment of recognition, Lyra fulfills her pledge to deliver the alethiometer to Lord Asriel and rescue Roger and the other stolen children—though with results that she finds, in the former instance, disappointing (Lord Asriel is stricken with a weird horror when he recognizes Lyra at the door of his polar fortress of solitude) and, in the latter, unexpectedly tragic, as poor Roger provides the means for Lord Asriel's breaching of the border between worlds.

The second volume, *The Subtle Knife*, introduces a new character, one who will come to assume an equal stature in the series to Lyra's. He is Will Parry, a boy of roughly Lyra's age who lives in a drab suburb near Oxford—our Oxford, this time. When we meet him, Will is struggling to protect himself and his mother—his father, an explorer and former Royal Marine, disappeared years before—from some sinister men, vaguely governmental, who are after the letters that Mr. Parry sent back home from the Arctic just before his disappearance. It's a struggle for Will because his mother is no help at all; she's mad, affected by some kind of obsessive-compulsive disorder that leaves her barely functional as a human being, let alone as a mother. For years, young Will has been handling all the duties and chores that his mother can't manage, and caring for her on her bad days, working very hard to maintain the illusion that all is well in the Parry house. He doesn't want them to come and take his mother away from him.

When the government agents grow overbold and confront his mother directly, Will realizes that his life is about to change. There is a poignant scene in which, seeking out the only kind, trustworthy person he has ever known—he has no friends—he leaves his bewildered mother with a nearly equally bewildered older woman who was once, briefly, his piano teacher, Mrs. Cooper (the name alludes to Susan Cooper, author of the beloved The Dark Is Rising sequence of novels, whose central protagonist is a boy named Will). Then he finds and collects his father's letters, accidentally killing one of the government men in the process, and flees.

He flees—though this is not, of course, his intention at first—into another world, to a place called Cittàgazze, the City of the Magpies. For it turns out that there are other ways to pass among the worlds than by Lord Asriel's costly method of child-sacrifice and trans-dimensional demolition. One can, if properly equipped, simply *cut* a hole in the membrane that separates realities from each other. To do this one needs a knife—a very special kind of knife, naturally: a subtle knife. There is only one of these in all the worlds; it was forged, some three hundred years ago, by the savants of the Torre degli Angeli, a kind of scientific academy housed in a castellated tower in Cittàgazze. They forged it; and then, unfortunately, they began to use it, cutting their way from world to world, leaving a trail of carelessly abandoned holes such as the one through which Will, fleeing the murder he has committed, tumbles.

In the desolate, di Chirico streets of Cittàgazze, Will Parry meets Lyra; she has come from her world through the breach Lord Asriel created, hoping to solve the riddle of Dust, intuiting that contrary to the teachings of the Church, it may in fact be a blessing and not a curse. Lyra is at first as startled to see a living, thriving boy with no dæmon as Will is to watch her pet cat transform itself into a stoat. But the two children, alone in a world of wild menacing orphans (all the adults here having fled or been devoured), form a bond, and make common cause: Will, following hints in John Parry's letters, intends to track his father down. And Lyra, taking instruction from the alethiometer, determines to help him. In an exciting scene Will inherits the subtle knife, and away the two children go, in search of John Parry and the riddle of Dust.

They are far from alone in these pursuits; a host of adult characters—Lee Scoresby, Iorek Byrnison, Mrs. Coulter, Lord Asriel, the witch Serafina Pekkala, a nun-turned-theoretical-physicist of our world named Mary Malone—follow courses that parallel, intersect with, or shadow Will and Lyra's. *The Golden Compass* is Lyra's book, structured around her and presented almost wholly through her point of view, and as such it reads very much like a traditional quest story. *The Subtle Knife*, with its shifting points of view and its frequent presentation of adult perspectives on Lyra and Will, has much more the flavor of a thriller. It is unflaggingly inventive, chilling and persuasive, has a number of gripping action sequences, and ends with a thrilling zeppelin battle in the Himalayas. But something—the pleasure inherent, perhaps, in the narrative unfolding of a single consciousness—is lost in the transition from first volume to second; and though Pullman's storytelling gifts reach their peak in *The Subtle Knife*, the sequence itself never quite recovers from this loss.

Nevertheless, the proliferation of points of view and different quests, which expands still farther in the third volume, *The Amber Spyglass*, is itself a kind of figure for the necessary loss of innocence, for the *felix culpa*, or Fortunate Fall, that lies at the heart of this deliberate, at times overdeliberate rejoinder or companion to *Paradise Lost*. As Lyra's dæmon comes ever closer to settling in its final form, the narrative itself grows ever more unsettled; for a single point of view is a child's point of view, but a multiple point of view is the world's. And the settling of a dæmon into a single form with the onset of adulthood, Pullman tells us, represents not simply a loss of the power to change, of flexibility and fire; it also represents a gain in the power to focus, to concentrate, to understand, and, finally, to accept: a gain in wisdom. Even Mrs. Coulter, that wicked, wicked woman, is granted her place in the narrative, and Pullman (not entirely successfully) makes us privy to her heart.

I have resisted trying to summarize, and thereby spoil, the vast, complicated plot of His Dark Materials, which runs to more than twelve hundred pages. But there is no way to form or convey a judgment of the sequence without giving away the name, alas, of the ultimate, underlying villain of the story, a character whose original scheme to enslave, control, and dominate all sentient life in the universe is threatened first by the implications of Dust as *felix culpa* and then by the ambition of the new Lucifer, Lord Asriel, with whose Second Rebellion the plot of *The Amber Spyglass* is largely concerned. The gentleman's name is Jehovah.

4.

The Amber Spyglass was awarded the *Guardian's* fiction prize for 2000, the first time that a novel ostensibly written for children had been so honored. Shortly afterward, the new laureate stirred up controversy by publicly attacking his fellow Oxonian C. S. Lewis, and in particular the Narnia books (which also begin, of course, in a wardrobe), calling them racist, misogynist, and allied with a repressive, patriarchal, idealist program designed to quash and devalue human beings and the world—the only world—in which we have no choice but to live and die.

Or something like that. I confess to taking as little interest in the question of organized Christianity's demerits as in that of its undoubted good points, in particular when such a debate gets into the works of a perfectly decent story and starts gumming things up. My heart sank as it began to dawn on me, around the time that the first angels begin to show up in *The Subtle Knife*, that there was some devil in Pullman, pitchfork-prodding him into adjusting his story to suit both the shape of his anti-Church argument (with which I largely sympathize) and the mounting sense of self-importance evident in the swollen (yet withal sketchy) bulk of the third volume and in the decreasing roundedness of its characters. By the end of the third volume, Lyra has lost nearly all the tragic, savage grace that makes her so engaging in *The Golden Compass*; she has succumbed to the fate of Paul Atreides, the bildungs-roman-hero-turned-messiah of Frank Herbert's science fiction novel *Dune*, existing only, finally, to fulfill the prophecy about her. She has harrowed Hell (a gloomy prison yard, according to Pullman, less Milton than Virgil, home of whispering ghosts cringing under the taunts and talons of the screws, a flock of unconvincing harpies), losing and then regaining her dæmon-soul; she has become, like all prophesied ones and messiahs, at once more and less than human.

This is a problem for Pullman, since His Dark Materials is explicitly—and materially, and often smashingly—about humanity. That's the trouble with Plot, and its gloomy consigliere, Theme. They are, in many ways, the enemy of Character, of "roundedness," insofar as our humanity and its convincing representation are constituted through contradiction, inconsistency, plurality of desire, absence of abstractable message or moral. It's telling that the epithet most frequently applied to God by the characters in His Dark Materials is "the Authority." This fits in well with Pullman's explicit juxtaposition of control and freedom, repression and rebellion, and with his championing of Sin, insofar as Sin equals Knowledge, over Obedience, insofar as that means the kind of incurious acceptance urged on Adam by Milton's Raphael. But the epithet also suggests, inevitably, the Author, and by the end of His Dark Materials one can't help feeling that Will and Lyra, Pullman's own Adam and Eve—appealing, vibrant, chaotic, disobedient, murderous—have been sacrificed to fulfill the hidden purposes of their creator. Plot is fate, and fate is always, by definition, inhuman.

Thank God, then, for the serpent, for the sheer, unstoppable storytelling drive that is independent of plot outlines and thematic schemes, the hidden story that comes snaking in through any ready crack when the Authority's attention is turned elsewhere. In *Paradise Lost*, we find ourselves, with Blake, rooting for the poets, for the "devil's party." Satan is one of us; so much more so than Adam or Eve. There's a puzzling pair of exchanges in *The Amber Spyglass*, when Lyra attempts to cheer the denizens at the outskirts of Hell, and sing for her supper, by telling them the story of her and Will's adventures up to that point. Like the accounts that Odysseus gives of himself, Lyra's is a near-total fabrication, replete with dukes and duchesses, lost fortunes, hair's-breadth escapes, ship-wrecks, and children suckled by wolves, and it's meant to be absurd, "nonsense"; but in fact it's made out of precisely the same materials, those dark materials of lies and adventure, as His Dark Materials. And the poor dwellers of the suburbs of the dead, listening to Lyra's tale, are comforted. It comes as a surprise, then, when having reached the land of the dead itself, Lyra's tale, with the apparent complicity of the narra-tor, is violently rejected by the Harpy, that humorless, bitter, inhuman stooge of God: "*Liar!*" Later, the Harpy hears Lyra's more accurate ac-count of her voyage and approves it, because, apparently, it sticks to the facts, and includes references to the substance of the corporeal world that the Harpy has never known. But so does the lie; and so, in spite of, or in addition to, its stated, anti-Narnian intentions, does His Dark Materials.

Lies, as Philip Pullman knows perfectly well, tell the truth; but the truth they tell may not be that, or not only that, which the liar intends. The secret story he has told is not one about the eternal battle between the forces of idealist fundamentalism and materialist humanism. It is a story about the ways in which adults betray children; how children are forced to pay the price of adult neglect, cynicism, ambition, and greed; how they are subjected to the programs of adults, to the general oblation board. Each of its child protagonists has been abandoned, in different ways, by both of his parents, and while they find no shortage of willing foster parents, ultimately they are betrayed and abandoned by their own bodies, forced into the adult world of compromise and self-discipline and self-sacrifice, or "oblation" in a way that Pullman wants us—and may we have the grace—to understand as not only inevitable but, on balance, a good thing.

Still, we can't help experiencing it—as we experience the end of so many wonderful, messy novels—as a thinning, a loss not so much of innocence as of wildness. In its depiction of Lyra's breathtaking liberty to roam the streets, fields, and catacombs of Oxford, free from adult supervision, and of Will's Harriet-the-Spy-like ability to pass, unnoticed and seeing everything, through the worlds of adults, a freedom and a facility that were once, but are no longer, within the reach of ordinary children; in simply taking the classic form of a novel that tells the story of children who adventure, on their own, far beyond the help or hindrance of grown-ups, His Dark Materials ends not as a riposte to Lewis or a crushing indictment of authoritarian dogma but as an invocation of the glory, and a lamentation for the loss, which I fear is irrevocable, of the idea of childhood as an adventure, a strange zone of liberty, walled, perhaps, but with plenty of holes for snakes to get in.

Michael Chabon is the author of two short story collections and four novels, including The Mysteries of Pittsburgh, Wonder Boys, The Amazing Adventures of Kavalier & Clay, *which won the Pulitzer Prize for Fiction in 2001, and the young adult novel* Summerland. *Originally published in* The Paris Review *and awarded its Aga Khan Prize, his most recent book is the novella* The Final Solution. *Chabon's work has appeared in such magazines as* The New Yorker, Harper's, GQ, Esquire, *and* Playboy, *and in a number of anthologies, among them* The O. Henry Prize Stories *and* Best American Short Stories. *He lives in Berkeley with his wife, Ayelet Waldman, also a novelist, and their four children.*

NAOMI WOOD

Dismembered Starlings and Neutered Minds
Innocence in His Dark Materials

Many people, when asked, say that childhood's most appealing trait is innocence. Associated with purity, with truth and with goodness, innocence is an essential part of all we say we value, something to be cherished, nurtured, protected. In the book of Genesis, innocence was irrevocably lost when Adam and Eve ate of the fruit of the tree of knowledge. Philip Pullman's His Dark Materials, however, asks not only that we re-evaluate our understanding of what innocence is but also our assumptions about what it means, whether it is, in fact, a quality to be valued.

In a 1997 review of Blake Morrison's book As If (an account of the pre-teen killers of the toddler James Bulger), Philip Pullman describes in horrifying detail how a gibbon at the zoo caught and tore apart a screaming starling, unemotionally, clinically: "I can't forget the crackings and snappings, the tough white sinews, the lolling shrieking head, and most of all the curious innocent concentration of the ape." By describing the ape's concentration as "innocent," Pullman highlights another aspect of innocence that few adults consider: its amorality. Although the ape may be said to be innocent in the sense that it has no moral consciousness to offend, its obliviousness does not negate the pain of the starling. The question raised for the human observer is the status of human consciousness, of conscience. When do humans become fully responsible for their actions? What does it mean to be innocent, to have experience? What makes humans human? Pullman's His Dark Materials explores these questions by asking readers to re-examine their notions of innocence in order to promote an alternate vision of the good from the one generally promoted by those who seek to preserve childhood innocence at any cost.

Although children have always been with us, the notion of childhood innocence—much more the notion that childhood innocence ought to be inviolable—is relatively recent. Puritans, after all, saw children, like adults, as irredeemably flawed by original sin and in as great a need of divine intervention as the most hardened criminal. In the seventeenth-century Puritans thought that human beings had been created good; however, Adam and Eve's sin in the Garden of Eden irrevocably marred all humanity. In the words of the New England Primer, "In Adam's Fall / We sinned all." With the rise of Enlightenment rationalism and Romanticism, new ideas about children became current. With John Locke, rationalists asserted that children were "tabula rasae," "blank slates," while Romantics such as Rousseau contended they were inherently good; both positions assumed children were marked for evil by their environments rather than their natures. By the time William Wordsworth wrote the Intimations Ode, asserting that children come into the world "trailing clouds of glory" dimmed only by the "prison-house" of experience, children and their innocence had become almost divine. Victorians went one step better than the Romantics by legislating childhood innocence and condemning those children deemed "not-childlike" as monstrous. These monstrous not-children tended to be those who had the misfortune to have their innocence destroyed because of their vulnerable socio-economic or racial status.

George Boas has traced this history of the "cult of childhood" and shown how it connects with anti-intellectualism, reactionary politics, and religious fervor. Judith Plotz has shown that in defining children as a species set apart from adults and childhood as a "vocation," some Romantics and Victorians created a terrible predicament for children such as Hartley Coleridge, son of Samuel Taylor Coleridge. Hartley's unenviable situation was to know that the farther he progressed away from the delightful "innocence" of his babyhood, the less appealing he was to his father. He appears to have spent the rest of his life trying to remain the spontaneous fairy-like baby his father had loved and celebrated in "Christabel," with inevitable contradictions splitting his psychic and physical identities as his body matured and experience told upon him.

As a student of Romantic and Victorian literature and the author of historical fiction set during the Victorian period (the Sally Lockhart series, among others), Philip Pullman is aware of the ways in which Victorian (and contemporary) overvaluation of innocence actually limits and even harms those whose innocence is ostensibly being protected. Pullman reread not only Milton's *Paradise Lost*, but also the works of William Blake in preparation for writing His Dark Materials, all studies of the meaning of good, evil, knowledge, and innocence. Blake's critique of innocence in the *Songs of Experience* (1792) demonstrates that although innocence may be briefly delightful, it is only a partial and imperfect state, defined more by what it is not than by what it is. Moreover, as Blake shows, experience exploits innocence, binding it unnaturally and cruelly, justifying its actions as do the parents in *Experience's* "Chimney Sweeper," who think because the child-sweep seems "happy, & dance[s] & sing[s], /... think they have done [him] no injury, / And are gone to praise God & his Priest & King, / Who make up a heaven of our misery" (ll. 9–12). Pullman, like Blake, traces the links between a God who attempts to deny humans full knowledge and the spiritual and temporal powers who police and exploit the boundaries between innocence and experience.

In *The Golden Compass*, Pullman subverts our notions of innocence by first showing children's innocence not as guiltless, but rather as uncouth, even feral—as the absence of knowledge and of culture rather than the presence of purity, love, or virtue. Lyra, the spirited heroine, is described initially as "a coarse and greedy little savage," a "half-wild cat." Her escapades include one very close to Pullman's description of the gibbon in the zoo: she tells Lord Asriel that when she and Roger, her bosom friend, found an injured rook on the library roof, she "was going to kill it and roast it but Roger said we should help it get better."[1] Lyra's unsentimental attitude toward the injured bird undercuts any sense that she has a natural affinity for nature, life, or virtue. And although adults may see children's play as "pleasant," "innocent and charming," children are actually just as political as their elders: Lyra is part of a "rich seething stew of alliances and enmities and feuds and treaties"; as leader of her own gang of children affiliated with Jordan College, she leads the others in "deadly warfare," delighting in physical combat and tactical victories. In her leadership ability, her physical courage, and her rhetorical power, Lyra possesses the same qualities as her parents, Lord Asriel and Mrs. Coulter, and has similar power to influence the people around her for good and ill. Being a child makes her no more inherently moral or immoral than any of the other individuals in the series.

---

[1] An even more explicit use of the gibbon episode is in the characterization of Mrs. Coulter's dæmon in *The Amber Spyglass*, p. 52.

Lyra begins to develop moral stature only with the gift of the alethi-ometer, the truth-telling device, and with the quest to rescue her friend Roger and other kidnapped children from the Gobblers, a slang term for the General Oblation Board and the most villainous ecclesiastical orga-nization of *The Golden Compass*. Lyra's parents have in their own way sought to keep her innocent—or at least, ignorant—of the greater battles being fought over human virtue and autonomy in this world; however, Lyra becomes an active participant in the struggle over the world's future only as her knowledge develops. The Master of Jordan College, knowing that he cannot warn Lyra of the dangers she will face or of the dread-ful danger Mrs. Coulter represents, gives her the alethiometer, which gives her the information she needs as she needs it. The gyptians give her knowledge of her parentage, Iorek Byrnison knowledge of bears, Se-rafina Pekkala knowledge of witches and even her father, Lord Asriel, knowledge of the origin of the Church's hatred and fear of Dust. All these things are crucial to her success in recognizing her parents for what they are, for regaining the bears' kingdom for Iorek and for reversing Dust's status and opposing the Church's mission to infantilize its believers by maintaining their innocence at all costs. Although the prophecy con-cerning Lyra decrees that she must accomplish her destiny in ignorance, her experiences and accrued knowledge over the course of the trilogy are crucial to her successful challenge of the doctrine of the primacy of in-nocence. Because the educational system in that world is so corrupted by the interference of the Church into matters of "experimental theology," or science, if Lyra were educated systematically she would never have the freedom to see the world as it is and might be.

The status and definition of Dust is the point of conflict between the forces seeking to preserve innocence and those who question it. Because Dust does not collect around children until after their dæmons are fixed, whereupon they become just as saturated with Dust as other adults, the Church has determined that it is physical evidence for Origi-nal Sin. In that world's Genesis, the Serpent promises Eve that with the eating of the fruit "your eyes shall be opened, and your dæmons shall assume their true forms, and ye shall be as gods, knowing good and evil." This world's Church has determined that such knowledge must be evil because it necessarily compromises the purity of innocence.

Working against knowledge for the preservation of innocence is the General Oblation Board, led by the redoubtable Mrs. Coulter. In bits and pieces we learn of Dust and of the General Oblation Board and its activities. We know that Dust has been the subject of debate among experimental theologians, some of whose discoveries have fundamentally challenged Church doctrines and definitions. The General Oblation Board works by stealth, stealing the children of the poorest and least powerful people of the country and taking them to Bolvanger in the remote north, where the unthinkable becomes not only thinkable but doable. In a grotesque and resonant parody of our world's science, Bolvanger institutes the practice of "intercision," the separation of children from their dæmons in order to preserve their innocence, even as Nazis and other eugenicists of the twentieth century sought to improve the human race by violating the deepest of human rights to self determination and autonomy. Lyra encounters the effects of the process at the instigation of the alethiometer: she finds Tony Makarios, shunned by fellow humans as an abomination, huddled in a frozen fish hut "clutching a piece of fish to him as Lyra was clutching Pantalaimon...but that was all he had, a piece of dried fish; because he had no dæmon at all. The Gobblers had cut it away. That was *intercision*, and this was a severed child." Lyra's horror and heroic self-mastery in order to treat Tony with compassion instead of repulsion testifies to her growing conscience and movement away from the amorality of innocence.

Mrs. Coulter attempts to justify the operation Lyra as something done "for the children's own good, my love. Dust is something bad, something wrong, something evil and wicked. Grown-ups and their dæmons are infected with Dust so deeply that it's too late for them. They can't be helped....But a quick operation on children means they're safe from it. Dust just won't stick to them ever again. They're safe and happy and —." Even Mrs. Coulter can't finish the thought. This assertion, that the General Oblation Board has only the best interests of children at heart when it performs the "little operation" to sever them from their dæmons, Lyra understands to be hollow. She has seen and knows too much: the pain of the parents whose children have been taken, the utter estrangement of Tony Makarios from human community, the pathetically caged dæmons, the empty eyes of the neutered hospital staff who no longer react to gross violations of children's fundamental humanity and her own feelings when she and Pantalaimon have themselves been threatened with the process. In preserving innocence, the Gobblers produce at best only mechanical people with neutered minds; at worst, they kill. Being severed from your dæmon may mean you won't be bothered with "all sort[s] of troublesome thoughts and feelings" about sex, but at the cost of any kind of human autonomy.

Pullman here expresses a rarely articulated aspect of the preservation of innocence. Most of the many censorship cases in the United States are for the purpose of preserving children's "innocence," or, in reality, their ignorance of things that might "scar" them—knowledge of such unfathomable atrocities as the Shoah, the effects of atomic bombs at Hiroshima and Nagasaki, the genocide of Native Americans, Australian Aboriginals, Armenians, Cambodians and Rwandan Tutsis. It is understandable that adults want to assure children (though we may doubt it ourselves) that humanity can be good as well as evil, despite these overwhelming historical events. More problematic, however, are the efforts to preserve children's ignorance of the knowledge that their own country may sometimes do the wrong thing, that even great leaders may be flawed. Most problematic of all, in the wake of the hullabaloo surrounding the exposure of a female nipple during the halftime show of the Superbowl in 2004, are the efforts to prevent children from knowing of the broad spectrum of human sexuality or even of the workings of their own bodies and how to protect or pleasure themselves. William Blake lamented the fetishization of sexual innocence two hundred years ago in many poems: in "The Garden of Love," the speaker sees that "where I used to play on the green" has been barred and shut, with "'Thou shalt not' writ over the door" and "Priests in black gowns...walking their rounds, / And binding with briars my joys & desires" (ll. 4, 6, 11–12). Pullman too shows that adults' fear of sexuality results in children's disenfranchisement from their human birthright, not only of sexuality but also of other kinds of knowledge.

Knowledge in general is conflated with sexuality and connected with pubescence in His Dark Materials as it has been in the history of Christianity. Pullman makes use of the traditional interpretation of the Fall and Original Sin as sexual when the Church in His Dark Materials connects Dust with pubescence. Sexuality is a fitting site for the contest between forces of purity and impurity because of its inescapably material, physical aspect, its connections with natural selection and its multifaceted nature. In contrast with a totalitarian mindset that privileges the One, the Pure, the Almighty, the Spiritual, sexuality with its anarchic subversion of intention, its messiness, its ability to overwhelm judgment and morality—even on the genetic level its unexpected and uncontrollable combinations of DNA—in all these things sexuality is the antithesis of purity and top-down order, and thus of the sort of innocence that requires ignorance and blankness. Pullman asks us to look at the forces demanding innocence and the costs of that demand.

Although sexuality is shown to be a crucial component of identity, it alone does not explain the phenomenon of Dust, nor does it become the *raison-d'être* of existence. Greater even than sexuality is self-consciousness: when "life becomes aware of itself," when humanity becomes able to judge between good and evil. In a sweeping synthesis of evolutionary theory, particle physics and human prehistory, His Dark Materials hypothesizes that something happened when humanity evolved the possibility of consciousness and that Dust is a part of that process. During her wanderings through multiple worlds, the earthly scientist Mary Malone comes to realize that there's a reason humans suddenly began creating art and making tools thirty thousand years ago, why various creatures in different places are conscious makers of culture and pattern—they respond to, are informed by and in turn generate Dust, the elemental matter of consciousness.

In contrast to the negative Eve-and-the-Serpent stories told in the Books of Genesis in his invented and our own world, Pullman's Mulefa recount the delight their own species' Eve experienced in becoming conscious. After taking the snake's advice to "Put your foot through the hole in the seedpod where I was playing, and you will become wise," the Mulefa-Eve wishes to "share it at once with her kindred. So she and her mate took the seedpods, and they discovered that they knew who they were, they knew they were Mulefa and not grazers. They gave each other names. They named themselves Mulefa...." Consciousness, for these creatures, is not a source of shame and guilt, but of joy. Pullman strongly suggests that to fall from innocence is not to become guilty, but simply to become conscious of responsibility as a sentient and moral being. Sin, shame and death come with consciousness not because consciousness is evil, but because we then understand our own actions and their potential effects upon others in a way we did not when we were innocent.

To discover Dust, then, is not to discover "God" in the sense that Dust is the primary mover or creator of the universe. Rather, Dust, or elementary particles—or "shadow particles" or "dark matter" or "sraf"— is one end of an evolutionary continuum, coalescing to become angels, attracted to the physical beings called humans. The Authority fears humans' independence because of their great physical strength combined with their consciousness, ability to reason, to imagine. With their ability to change and grow as well as their physical ability to manipulate their environment, they have the power to challenge the Authority and his dictates. Consciousness, then, aligns with sexuality in that connecting spiritual awareness with physical nature, sexual nature with the mind;

the Fall may result in conscious adults who are thoughtful and empathetic moral agents.

The Church's fear of sexuality overshadows the real task of adulthood: to become conscious and moral agents in a complex world that requires all our knowledge, reason and compassion. Encountering the universe with only a set of maxims about purity is no adequate way of understanding the dizzyingly various possibilities of life, culture, and choice. A case in point is the menacing and ultimately absurd assassin-missionary Father Gomez, who is commissioned to kill Lyra, a new Eve in the edenic—though post-lapsarian—world of the Mulefa, before she has a chance to fall into adulthood through sexuality. When he realizes this world to which he's come is full of sentient beings radically different from himself, his first thought is that they must be taught "that their habit of riding on wheels was abominable and Satanic, and contrary to the will of God. Break them of that, and salvation would follow." Like so many missionaries before him, Father Gomez does not consider the possibility of alternate ways of being good, of alternate ways of being in touch with God or the cosmos.

Sexuality is nature's way of ensuring change and growth; if in the "Fall" Eve and, through Eve, humanity accepted the challenge to recognize the difference between good and evil and thus separate themselves from the fabric of material existence, they also incurred a great responsibility to learn, to balance, to respect and to know. Such knowledge does not come easily, as Lyra learns when her intuitive ability to read the alethiometer leaves her along with her childhood. Instead, in the arduous process of re-learning the lost grace of childhood and replacing it with the knowledge of experience, innocence must become, fittingly, a toy unfit for conscious—and conscientious—adulthood.

Naomi Wood teaches children's and adolescent literature and Victorian novel courses at Kansas State University, where she is an associate professor of English. She is enthralled by fantasy writing, past and present, and has written about both British and American fantasy authors for academic journals. She admires Philip Pullman's challenges to unthinking piety and his deeply aesthetic and philosophical sense of story.

Works Cited

Boas, George. *The Cult of Childhood*. Studies of the Warburg Institute, vol. 29. London: The Warburg Institute, University of London, 1966.

Plotz, Judith. *Romanticism and the Vocation of Childhood*. New York: Palgrave, 2001.

Pullman, Philip. *The Amber Spyglass*. New York: Alfred A. Knopf, 2000.

———. *The Golden Compass*. Published in the U.K. as *Northern Lights*. New York: Alfred A. Knopf, 1995.

———. *The Subtle Knife*. New York: Alfred A. Knopf, 1997.

———. "Understand a Little More: Review of *As If*, by Blake Morrison." *The Independent*. 1 Feb. 1997. 6.

Sharkey, Alix. "Heaven, Hell, and the Hut at the Bottom of the Garden." Interview with Philip Pullman. *The Independent*. 6 December 1998. Features: 13.

His Dark Pharmaceuticals
Drug-related Themes and Imagery in the His Dark Materials Trilogy

Philip Pullman, the author of *The Golden Compass, The Subtle Knife* and *The Amber Spyglass,* was born in 1946. A graduate of Oxford, he currently lives in England.

This means that in 1967—the Summer of Love—he was presumably a twenty-one-year-old university student living a short drive away from London.

Hmmm.

Now, I don't mean to imply he was some sort of counter-culture, tie-dyed, drug-crazed freak—but even in the cloistered environs of Oxford, he must have *known* a few. London was a pretty swinging place in those days, and I'm sure he spent a weekend or two immersed in the *zeitgeist* of his time.

From all reports it was pretty good *zeitgeist*...freely available, gave you a real strong buzz, and usually laced with all sorts of questions about the nature of reality.

The question is, did it influence his writing—and if so, how?

Light My Fire, Feed Your Head

"If the doors of perception were cleansed, everything would appear to man as it is: infinite."

—WILLIAM BLAKE, *The Marriage of Heaven and Hell*

Blake is one of the influences Pullman mentions in the acknowledgements for *The Amber Spyglass*. This quote is where the psychedelic band the Doors got their name, and was also used as a title by Aldous Huxley. The "doors of perception" are clearly the senses, but what it means for them to be "cleansed" is open to discussion. . . and if you were talking to Jim Morrison, that discussion would probably be about the best way to get high.

There's plenty of historical precedent for using drugs as a perception-altering tool—and it's exactly that approach, that drugs are a tool, that Pullman uses throughout His Dark Materials.

Smokin' in the Old Boy's Room

In the very first chapter of *The Golden Compass*, we have a reference to something known as "leaf." It's valuable enough for the butler to swipe some...but eventually, it becomes apparent from context that this is the equivalent of tobacco. I say "eventually," because it's not *obviously* tobacco; Pullman does introduce both tobacco and "tabaco" later on, as well as cigars, cigarettes, and cigarillos. So why doesn't he just identify it up front?

Two reasons. First, he's establishing cultural differences between parallel worlds; Lyra's world uses one term for the substance, Will's world uses another, and a third world just changes the spelling.

Second, he's teasing us. He knows perfectly well the conclusion many adults will leap to, and he lets us make that jump. The reference is deliberate, and so are the ones that follow—meaning that Pullman's agenda may be more subversive than simply taking an adversarial stand against organized religion.

Even socially accepted drugs take on a counter-culture significance when applied to children. Lyra shows off her rebellious nature in *The Golden Compass*, when she and two "brat companions" pass a stolen cigarette between them, "blowing out the smoke ostentatiously." The detail helps establish Lyra's outlaw nature, both her adventurousness and disdain for other's rules.

Mother's Little Caffeinated Helper

Will's character is illustrated in the same way, but with a different drug: he's shown drinking coffee, which makes him seem more adult and responsible. Coffee is what grown-ups drink in the morning so they can go to work, and that's exactly the kind of person Will is—reliable and hard-working.

When Lyra goes to see Mary Malone, the doctor is extremely tired and makes herself some instant coffee to wake herself up while Lyra talks. What Lyra tells her changes Mary's life forever; the coffee is a metaphor for Mary literally waking up to a new world.

Considering that Pullman is British, you'd think tea would be more prevalent than coffee—but oddly enough, it doesn't even make an appearance until the third book, in the scene where Mrs. Coulter has just finished drugging Lyra:

> Nevertheless, his skepticism affected her, and as she crumbled the dark gray tea brick into the water, she wondered what in the world she thought she was doing, and whether she had gone mad, and, over and over again, what would happen when the Church found out. The Golden Monkey was right. She wasn't only hiding Lyra: she was hiding her own eyes.

The tea is an important symbol here for several reasons. On one level, it contrasts what Mrs. Coulter has just done to her own daughter—Lyra slumbers in a drugged sleep while Mrs. Coulter makes tea to keep herself awake.

More importantly though, it represents stability, both in the solid nature of the brick of tea and in the comforting, familiar behavior it invokes. And as the "dark gray tea brick" crumbles, we can see Mrs. Coulter's self-assurance doing the same; she no longer views her own actions in the clear, black-and-white way she used to. The tea is her attempt to regain some composure through the ritual use of a drug.

Tea shows up again when Lyra and Will are in the town of the dead, a place dreary and dismal in every way. They are given "thin, dry bread" and "bitter tea," which is all the dead have to offer them; the solace of a familiar, soothing beverage becomes the exact opposite, heightening the sense of desolation and hopelessness.

The last appearance of tea is also Will's final scene, and the last thing we hear Dr. Mary Malone say:

> "My flat's about half a mile away, and you know what I'd like most of all in the world? I'd like a cup of tea. Come on, let's go and put the kettle on."

With these words, she and Will return to the ordinary world and ordinary life. Tea no longer represents a counterpoint to chaos or despair; it has regained its status as a symbol of normalcy and comfort.

One Tokay Over the Line, Sweet Jesus

Of course, normalcy is a tricky concept, and comfort can be treacherous. After a heady day of shopping and a luxurious bath, Mrs. Coulter puts Lyra to bed after giving her "a warm drink with milk and herbs," foreshadowing her eventual drugging of Lyra to keep her captive.

Nor is it the first time that drugs are used to entice, lull and control children. Offers of chocolatl, a "sweet, hot liquor," is the inducement Mrs. Coulter employs to lure children into her grasp so they can be shipped off for medical experiments. Pullman could have simply used hot chocolate; his description of the drink as alcoholic is deliberate.

Alcohol is neither demonized nor praised in His Dark Materials. Its use depends on context. At a cocktail party it's just part of the background, while the "Jenniver spirit" of the gyptians or Lee Scoresby's preference for bourbon whisky are cultural details. Brandy is used as a medical aid when Will hurts his hand, and a tool for illicit seduction when a lecherous old man tries to spike Lyra's coffee with it.

Alcohol crops up again and again in the trilogy as both metaphor and plot device; it actually plays a favorable role in one of the most important scenes of all, when Dr. Malone tells Lyra the story of how she gave up being a nun. While it is the taste of marzipan, "a bit of some sweet stuff," that reminds the doctor of her first love and triggers her decision to leave the church, she freely admits that the wine she was drinking may have influenced her, too—and she doesn't care. The implication is that the wine didn't cloud her judgment, it merely made her more receptive to the truth.

Alcohol, of course, can be used to numb as well as enlighten. The great armored bear, Iorek Byrnison, drinks to dull the pain of having his armor stolen. "I want it back," he says, "and then I shall never need spirits again." Iorek is a warrior, a professional killer by trade; his consuming of "raw spirits" can also be seen as a metaphorical pun on taking lives. The parallel between the two meanings of "spirits" is even more pronounced in the Suburbs of the Dead, where the Gallivespians are given glasses of a "clear and pungent spirit" while surrounded by those very close to death itself.

Vodka is the central metaphor in Chapter Eight of *The Amber Spyglass*, a chapter named after the drink itself. Will meets a priest, who is obviously interested in him for sexual reasons. Like the man who tries to give Lyra brandy, the priest presses Will to drink a glass of vodka. He complies, but is almost overcome by nausea and promises himself he will never drink vodka again. Closely paralleling the poisoned bottle of Tokay, here alcohol symbolizes corruption and vice, specifically in the context of organized religion.

I Got Comfortably Numb, and I Missed It

Lee Scoresby also uses vodka to loosen an associate's tongue and gain valuable information, including this description of Will's father, Stanislaus Grumman:

> "Instead of using regular medicines, he insisted on using the stuff the bears use—bloodmoss—some kind of lichen, it ain't a true moss."

Bloodmoss is pivotal, being the substance that Grumman turns into an ointment that winds up saving Will's life. The fact that it's made from a lichen, though it might seem a trivial detail, is significant; ergot, the naturally occurring source of LSD, is also a lichen.

Then there's the combination of cigar smoke and "jimsonweed ointment" Lee Scoresby uses to keep insects at bay—jimson weed, also known as Angel's Trumpet and Devil's Trumpet, is related to belladonna and has a long history as a hallucinogen used for religious purposes.

Both of these substances, though portrayed in strictly medical terms, have links to drugs used for more mind-altering reasons. The third, and most powerful, example of this is in the operation of the separator, a sort of psychic guillotine. This is how it's described by one of the doctors:

> "But the first big breakthrough was the use of anesthesia combined with the Maystadt anbaric scalpel. We were able to reduce death from operative shock to below five percent."

Once again, it is a drug that enables an important part of the plot to proceed, by making the pain of a horrific process bearable. The process itself is more than mind-altering—it is soul-altering, permanently severing the link between a child and his dæmon. At this point, the drug-related symbolism begins to take on overtones that are more metaphysical than metaphoric.

Puff the Magic Dæmon

Another metaphysical drug is cedarwood, which has a soporific effect on dæmons; it does not have to be ingested—it merely has to be present. This is also apparently enough to confuse the senses of dæmons, enough that they cannot locate a concealed Lyra. Since dæmons are a physical representation of a person's soul—or a facet thereof—it is the soul itself that is being deceived by the cedarwood.

Drugs and magic are combined when the witch Serafina Pekkala treats Will's wounded hand: "This will need more than herbs to heal. It will need a spell." She then gives Will "a little horn cup containing a hot potion whose bitterness was moderated by honey, and presently he lay back and fell deeply asleep."

Drugs are used many times in the trilogy to knock people out. When Lyra is captured and taken to the Experimental Station, she's given drugged milk to put her to sleep. And of course, her own mother, Mrs. Coulter, keeps her sedated for days with this concoction:

> "Crouching down, she crumbled some dried leaves into it, two pinches from this bag, one from that, and added three drops of a pale yellow oil."

Note that she doesn't inject Lyra or give her pills—she uses dried leaves from a bag, which sounds suspiciously like marijuana. The pale yellow oil fits the description of honey oil, a powerful distilled form of hashish.

Hey, Jude—What Did You Put in My Drink?

Poison can symbolize many things. In *The Amber Spyglass* the cries of the Harpies are described as, "... high, mournful shrieks and wails that hung in the air like the drifting filaments of a jellyfish, causing pain wherever they touched."

However, it's most often used as a metaphor for betrayal: a noxious substance, secretly added to something that usually gives pleasure, and served to the victim by someone close to them. While people ingest various substances deliberately in His Dark Materials, just as often they are given them surreptitiously or against their will. This is true of the wine Mrs. Coulter poisons Carlo with in *The Subtle Knife* after pumping him for information, or any of the drugs she gives Lyra to control her.

The Gallivespians have poisoned spurs on their legs they use to kill their enemies—poison that not only produces intense pain, but hallucinations, as well. Even the Kingdom of Heaven employs "poison-spraying cannons"—perhaps a pun on the word "canon," meaning an established set of rules.

The incident that starts the whole story moving is when Lyra spots the Master poisoning a bottle of Tokay wine. An important distinction must be made here, however: it isn't the wine *itself* that's a symbol of evil—it's the betrayal of the poison that's important. Wine is used by the Catholic Church to represent the blood of Christ; poisoned wine, therefore, can be seen as symbolizing the corruption of Christ's teachings. In a larger sense, it can be even be seen as representing the betrayal of religion itself—something that is supposed to give comfort, given to us by people we trust, but ultimately poisonous.

I've Got Drugs in My Parka, and I Don't Know What to Do with Them

Iorek Byrnison is supposed to be the king of the bears. Instead, he's exiled after killing another bear in a fight over a female. Normally, the weaker of two bears in combat eventually recognizes the fact and surrenders, but Iorek's opponent does not; it is theorized that he's been given "confusing herbs" that cloud his judgment and make him fight until he is killed.

Pullman's references to drugs are fairly cautious throughout—necessary, since the trilogy is aimed at the young adult audience—but here he ventures into more dangerous territory. Alcohol, tobacco or caffeine are socially accepted, as are pharmaceuticals in the service of medicine, or even poison as a plot device. But "confusing" is just a euphemism for psychoactive—whatever the "herbs" were, they got that bear *high*.

And bears aren't the only ones. In the second chapter of *The Golden Compass*, the Master cuts up and sautés some poppy heads, preparing them to be served to the other Scholars. Poppies, of course, are the source of opium—and it's the actual head of the plant that the drug is collected from. The flowers are introduced in the same paragraph as the decanters of booze and racks of pipes laid out for the pleasure of the Scholars, the implication being that poppy heads occupy the same sort of niche as the other accepted vices.

Pullman isn't the first author to appropriate poppies as a symbol in a children's book; Frank L. Baum used a field of them in *The Wizard of Oz* to put his characters to sleep. But Pullman's poppy heads aren't there as a sedative:

> "Poppy was always served after a feast; it clarified the mind and stimulated the tongue, and made for rich conversation."

This is a highly significant passage. We're being told that the intellectual elite of this world regularly take a powerful, mind-altering drug…because it *enhances* their mental faculties. And this is not an illegal or unsavory practice, either; it is a ritual as established and accepted as brandy and cigars after dinner.

Another drug that pops up as a stimulant is the "soft, bitter-tasting leaves" that the witch Serafina Pekkala gives to Will. They warm him up and make him more alert, which is the reason Peruvian Indians chew on coca leaves—the source of cocaine—while hiking at high altitudes.

An even more obvious parallel is the powder used to wake Lyra from her drugged sleep. The shaman that mixes it gives instructions that it be administered "into the nostrils of the sleeping child a little at a time." Out of all the methods Pullman could have used to deliver a stimulant, he chose a powder inhaled through the nose—he even has it wrapped in a little bindle of folded paper, a detail as familiar to many drug-users as the razor-blade, the mirror and the rolled-up hundred-dollar bill.

He can get away with this largely because opium and cocaine are more sophisticated, adult drugs—children, even teens, are less likely to spot the symbolism. When it comes to substances that are smoked, though, he has to be more careful, which is probaby why "smokeweed" is only mentioned once, very briefly, in *The Subtle Knife*:

> "My respects to you and your tribe," Lee said. "I have some smokeweed, which is not worthy, but I would be honored to present it to you."

Having established that tobacco is called smokeleaf in Lyra's world, this variant—a gift to a shaman—is no doubt meant to be marijuana, "weed" being a common slang term from the sixties.

Shamans, of course, have a long history of altering their own consciousness. Stanislaus Grumman, Will's father, is initiated into a Tartar tribe called the Yenisei Pakhtars by having a hole drilled in his skull. This process, called trepanning, is done more to acknowledge the fact that Grumman is already a shaman than to make him one. Trepanning is the oldest surgical technique known, with some trepanned skulls dating back to 3000 B.C.; it was done for various reasons, ranging from curing headaches to releasing evil spirits from the brain.

When Lyra uses her alethiometer in a museum to ask why an ancient skull had been trepanned, she discovers the skull belonged to a sorcerer and that the hole had been made to let the gods into his head. A man that strikes up a conversation with her about the skull tells her this about trepanning:

> "D'you know, people still do that?"
> "Yeah," she said.
> "Hippies, you know, people like that. Actually you're far too young to remember hippies. They say it's more effective than taking drugs."

So, as with other shamanic practices, the purpose of trepanning in this case seems to be to alter consciousness for mystical reasons. The mention of hippies is also important; it reminds us that despite all the talk of alternate worlds and magic, the social revolution of the sixties is still part of the fabric of this universe.

When Lyra finds out that the substance known as Dust is concentrated more heavily along the edges of the hole in the skull, another convergence of the magical and the mind-expanding is confirmed.

Everything Must Get Stoned

When a dying angel is brought before him, Lord Asriel throws a handful of herbs on a brazier; the smoke has the effect of defining the angel's fading body more clearly. Not only that, but the angel finds that inhaling the smoke of the herbs gives him the strength to hang on. The chemical and the divine come together again.

Angels, we discover, are made of Dust, also known as Shadows, Dark Matter or *sraf*, the cosmic particle at the conceptual heart of His Dark Materials. It is attracted to sentience and the products of sentience, and accumulates in higher concentrations in adults than children. Dust, we eventually learn, are particles of consciousness itself, present since the beginning of the universe. They either evolved or were shaped into angels, a form of life not based on solid matter. As with organic life, there are many kinds of angels, and the civilization they construct is eventually ruled over by a central power called the Authority. The Authority is not God the Creator—he's God the Dictator. When the inevitable revolution arrives and fails, the rebel angels manipulate the evolution of organic life in order to produce consciousness, creating allies in their battle for free will.

In the case of the alien race called the Mulefa, the angels do so by impregnating the oil of a certain kind of seed-pod with their own essence, particles of Dust. When Dr. Mary Malone asks about the relationship between the oil and the Mulefa, she's told a variation on the Adam and Eve story, where the creatures attain consciousness through their exposure to it:

> "And the oil entered her blood and helped her see more clearly than before, and the first thing she saw was the sraf."

The sraf is their name for Dust, as well as being a word that sounds a lot like seraph, a type of angel. But it is the oil that is important here, because it changes the symbolism of an apple (or according to some interpretations, a pomegranate) being eaten to an oil being absorbed into the bloodstream. By doing so, it makes the metaphor much clearer; we suddenly see both the apple and the oil for what they are, tools for expanding consciousness... or in other words, drugs.

Not only does this illustrate that drugs are tools, it also shows that metaphorically, tools can be drugs. The oil is also used as a lubricant for the Mulefa's wheels, a wheel being one of the most basic and important tools that exist. If we use the definition that a drug is something that alters our perception of the world, causing us to think in a different way, then the namesakes of all three books in the trilogy—*The Golden Compass*, *The Subtle Knife* and *The Amber Spyglass*—are all symbols for drugs.

Lyra in the Sky with Diamonds

The alethiometer of *The Golden Compass* might seem at first like a glorified crystal ball, but its function isn't to tell the future; it's to tell the truth. And in order to use it properly, you must be in a specific state of mind:

> "Remembering what Farder Coram had said, she tried to focus her mind on three symbols taken at random, and clicked the hands round to point at them, and found that if she held the alethiometer just so in her palms and gazed at it in a particularly lazy way, as she thought of it, the long needle would begin to move more purposefully."

This "particularly lazy way" is the same kind of unfocused state that many people find to be when they get their most creative ideas. It can occur when you're falling asleep, waking up, or daydreaming...or under the influence of certain drugs. At such times previously unsuspected connections between concepts will suddenly be made clear, and understanding will crystallize. It is exactly this principle that the alethiometer is based on, connecting concepts represented by the device's symbols to present a coherent message. It generates not just truth, but inspiration.

And what powers this inspiration? Dust, the particles of consciousness that symbolize the intelligence of the universe itself, the cosmic mentality. The underlying theme here is that a receptive frame of mind will receive truth in the form of inspiration, from the universe itself—an endorsement for altered consciousness as a means of enlightenment.

I Can See Clearly Now, My Brain Is Gone

In order to create the amber spyglass, Dr. Mary Malone realizes she will have to cultivate the same unfocused state of mind that Lyra uses to read the alethiometer. When she does so, she comes up with the idea to create lenses from hardened sap, and eventually discovers that coating them with Dust-impregnated oil allows her to actually see particles of Dust in the air. This shift in her perceptions leads her to a much greater understanding of how the universe actually works.

The spyglass represents the "doors of perception." In his poem Blake uses the metaphor of acid dissolving false perceptions and leaving only truth; Pullman has Dr. Malone use acid in her attempts to scour the lenses clean of imperfections. She succeeds, and is rewarded with being able to see one of the fundamental forces of existence—a glimpse of the infinite. A drug—the oil of consciousness—has directly affected her perceptions, and permanently changed the way she thinks.

The First Snort Is the Deepest

The way drugs are used determine how they're viewed. Drugs used as medicine are benevolent; drugs used to harm are evil. Drugs used to alter perception, though, occupy a gray area; they can be seen as either, or both.

What matters is *intent*, the effect the user—or the giver—of the drug means to induce. This might seem obvious... but Pullman's insight goes deeper than that. He recognizes that tools *themselves* have intent, that despite the best motives of their users, certain things are inherently dangerous. Some drugs are, by their natures, poisonous or addictive—and some tools are made to destroy, not create.

The eponymous blade of *The Subtle Knife* does both. At first it seems an instrument of creation, able to open portals between worlds—it's not until the end of the trilogy we discover that these dimensional wounds have been bleeding Dust, the life-force of existence. The knife is also responsible for the creation of the Specters, the soul-consuming phantoms that prey on the living.

The knife is still a drug metaphor, but not for the unfocused, dreamlike frame of mind represented by the alethiometer or the spyglass. The knife stands for the exact opposite, the double-edged blade of drugs like cocaine or amphetamines. The knife requires intense concentration to wield, and while a powerful weapon, its use is eventually revealed to carry a very high price. It creates hungry, soulless monsters—potent symbols of addiction.

Dust in the Mind

The Church believes Dust to be Original Sin, the physical embodiment of the first and greatest mistake ever made by Mankind. By eating the forbidden fruit, Adam and Eve aren't just disobeying their creator; they're acquiring self-awareness, symbolized by their sudden knowledge of their own nakedness. For the first time, humans are capable of making choices—not just acting, but picking one path over another through a consideration of the consequences. In Pullman's eyes, this is one of the defining characteristics of adulthood, the difference between the impulsiveness of the young and the deliberation of the mature. This is why Dust is attracted to adults more than children, and also to manmade artifacts; both are imbued with *intention*, the focusing of will through intellect and informed by emotion.

Together, these elements define consciousness; separately, they define the main characters. Will is obviously the embodiment of his namesake; his steadfast, stubborn nature provides half the equation, while Lyra's adaptable, passionate personality—her name, so close to "lyrical," evoking the emotional complexity of music—provides the other.

If Will and Lyra represent a single, metaphorical mind, then Dust is a universal, metaphorical drug—not original sin, but original spirit. Spirit in this sense is the universal life-force that connects all things; Dust is found everywhere. The reason it's found in higher concentrations in sentient beings or their creations is because it's attracted to itself, clustering together much the same way matter does through gravity or other natural forces. Spirit is attracted to spirit, consciousness is attracted to consciousness, and more and more self-awareness is thereby generated.

The inevitable result of this process of self-awareness and attraction is love. Love is the awareness of not only your own spirit, but of that same spirit in others and the desire to be closer to it. When Will and Lyra fall in love, it is the uniting of two halves of the same symbolic consciousness, and this union attracts such an outpouring of Dust that a great disaster is averted. And here the metaphor comes full circle, for it is now the consciousness affecting the drug; it is their full-blown *awareness* of each other that diverts the sentience of the universe away from the despair of the Abyss.

As with many drugs, the effect is only temporary, and comes at a price—Lyra and Will cannot stay together. But then, certain drugs aren't meant to last forever. They're there to provide a temporary boost, or respite or change in perspective. They're a tool, able to cause harm or illuminate truth depending on how they're used.

Much like a knife, an alethiometer, a spyglass...or a work of fiction.

Don DeBrandt is a writer from Vancouver, BC, with five published science fiction novels. He also writes crime fiction under the pseudonym Donn Cortez, including the thriller The Closer, *forthcoming mystery* The Man Burns Tonight, *and two* CSI: Miami *novels,* The Body System *and* Riptide.

SARAH ZETTEL

Dust to Dust

The Destruction of Fantasy Trope and Archetype in His Dark Materials

I stumbled across *The Golden Compass* by chance, which I suppose is appropriate. I picked it up in the bookstore. I liked the cover, I liked the blurb, I really liked the little bit I read standing in front of the display. I took it home and was quickly enraptured. The story was exciting, the characters gripping, the heroes complex and the villains really, really villainous.

It was not until I'd read the two sequels and considered the work as a whole that I understood some of what Philip Pullman had done to make the first book in particular so special. He tackled head-on a number of the most pervasive fantasy tropes and archetypes and took them apart. In fact, he ground some of them into Dust.

For an author there a risk in doing this. The reason trope and archetype exist is that they are well-understood by the reader, they have a strong emotional resonance, or both. For an author to successfully take them apart, they must provide something strong and clear for a replacement. Otherwise, the story is going to be emotionally confusing and dissatisfying. Unfortunately, Pullman does not entirely succeed in this last, vital task with his story and it weakens the whole of this ambitious work.

Pullman is at his best when dealing with some of the weakest and least examined fantasy tropes. He starts with one of my least favorite: the Girl-Animal Telepathic Bond.

You know, in some ways I shouldn't be a fantasy fan. I have never once—not in my private musings, not in my juvenile writings—fantasized about having a telepathic bond with an animal. I have never wanted a horse, hawk, cat (you notice, it's never a dog?) or wolf who instantly knew everything I was thinking and feeling. For one thing, do you actually want your cat to know what you're thinking when you boot it across the room because it's on the table licking the butter again? Or, worse, do you want to know what your *cat* is thinking at this moment?

Of course, fantasy telepathic animals are never really animals. They're furry people, and that, to me, makes the whole trope even more disturbing. Another person in my head? All the time? No privacy, no chance to think or feel for myself? No secrets?

No way.

Yes, I read and loved Anne McCaffrey's dragons of Pern with their mental and emotional bonds to their riders—until I stopped to think about them. In McCaffrey's work you are completely out of control. The dragon chooses you, whether you want it or not. Of course, no one in her stories would possibly turn down this magnificent bond, 'cause of course, you're not going to be chosen unless you're really destined for it, which is all part of the fantasy. But the control of self and body goes even further, because when your dragon is ready to have sex, you are going to have sex with the human partner of whatever dragon they end up mating with. Your ability, your very desire to say no is completely eradicated. Of course, all dragon riders are nice people, and there don't seem to be any sibling or parental combination problems here. If there are, the author is not talking about it.

But I can't help thinking about it, and as soon as I do there goes the fantasy.

Now, Pullman's version of the bond removes all the above problems. Instead of shackling two independent beings together because of some greater destiny, he presents the bond as two portions of the same soul. The dæmon is not only the conscience of the human; it is the manifestation of self-love. The dæmons love their humans and are loved in return. In Lyra's world not even the poorest street child is completely alone and unloved. They have their dæmon to love them, advise them, be with them when there is no one else. Thus, the depth of the horror that Mrs. Coulter and the others perpetrate removes from these children that last and greatest love.

Pullman also beautifully remakes the cliché of the Talking Animal. Fantasy is loaded with talking animals. Fantasy animals are downright chatty! This is understandable, as fantasy's roots are in fairy tales, and in fairy tales, animals talk. In fact, in a traditional fairy tale, if you don't listen to the talking animal you can end up very dead.

In modern fantasy, however, we generally see the talking animal singularly. They are not truly animals with separate desires and alien needs. Like their telepathic relatives, they are furry people, content to help humans on their various quests.

Pullman turns this cliché on its head with an elegant, two-part solution. First, he give the panserbjorn a society. He creates a culture, so that the reader has a reference and an *explanation* for Iorek. He shows us what the fighting bears are like when there are no humans around. We are shown their separate, alien existence, and we are shown that they are frightening. Bears are not friendly, they are not cuddly and they are not safe even when they like you. They are polar bears, really big predators—and Pullman does not let us forget that, a fact for which I applaud him.

We are also shown, in a wonderful and simple exchange about feeling cold, that Iorek has no concept of what it is to *be* human and isn't particularly interested in gaining one. In fact the desire to be a human is Iofur's insane weaknes, something Lyra plays up to her advantage.

But Pullman doesn't stop there. He also overturns the usual fantasy-novel denouement for Lyra's relationship with Iorek. Generally in modern fantasy the talking animals must either die or give up the rest of their independent lives to be with the heroine (which tends to become the major focus of the sequel). To have the intense relationship between Lyra and Iorek end in both of them going contentedly and purposefully on their own ways is highly unusual, as is the fact that Iorek is never made out to be a sidekick. Iorek from the first has his own goals and his own life to resume. He begins as an independent figure and he remains one until the end.

In fact, there is an admirable lack of sidekicks in the series. Each character has individual priorities and motivations. All fellowships are temporary, separated or driven together by the diverse goals of the characters. Even true love has a temporary nature: oddly enough for a fantasy this does not lead to tragedy, but salvation.

Pullman's work also provides an interesting take on the prevalent idea that a creature in a fantasy novel must be true to its biological nature. One of my fellow fantasy authors insists that fantasy is inherently racist because each race of beings is given a set of behavioral traits that are permanently and unchangingly theirs by virtue of being a member of their race. All dwarves are grumpy and greedy, all elves are wise, and so on. My author friend argues that this takes the aspect of racism that human beings of different "races" have differing inherent character traits, and makes it true.

Now, I'm not certain I buy this argument in its entirety, but it does provide an extra insight into some of the oversimplification of character that can occur in fantasy.

While Pullman does incorporate this idea of inherent traits of a race or species, he does it in a different way. First, intelligence always trumps biology in his fantastic races. When he creates a rational being he gives it sound emotional and intellectual intelligence. No member of a Pullman race is always any one thing. They are each individuals within their own race or culture. Second, he uses the biological differences between his races as part of his thesis against organized religion. He makes the Magisterium racist. The Magisterium makes no allowance for difference of behavior, even in the case of difference in physical makeup. This irrational intransigence helps show the Church up for the evil Pullman is making it out to be.

Let me tell you, speaking as an author, this is tough to do.

However, one of the most formidable tropes Pullman takes on in His Dark Materials is love. Love is a major theme in fantasy. Love is credited for saving more worlds and more lives than just about anything else. It's up there with honor and a good right hook. But for most authors, me included, it's violence, that good right hook, that really saves the day. The bad guy is killed good and dead and the hero who managed to get him that way can ride off into the sunset.

Philip Pullman does not do that, and to me that is one of the most remarkable aspects of the series. Love not only literally makes the world go round—it saves the day. Love is the most powerful force in the universe. It is more powerful than God and all the angels bright or dark, and Pullman spins this into the most original fantasy denouement since Tolkein.

Okay, now I'm in cliché territory, I know, but bear with me for a minute.

I am not the world's greatest Tolkein fan; however, some things that Tolkein did no one else has been able to come close to. One of them is the underlying reason for the salvation of Middle Earth, which is saved from Sauron and the Ring because of an act of mercy. In *The Hobbit* Bilbo could have killed Gollum, but he didn't. He "stayed his hand." It was mercy and it was pity, which more than any other saved the world. Bilbo's mercy inspired Frodo's mercy, which left Gollum alive to destroy the Ring when Frodo failed.

Mercy saved the world. Not violence, not the sword from the stone or the bolt from above. Mercy.

In Pullman, it is love, and an act of love between two human beings that saves all. Not violence, not the threat or promise of violence. Not power, but love, pure and far from simple. He sets it up and he carries it through. Love is the ultimate good, and passionate love is an integral part of that good.

I like Pullman's use of the power of love even better since George Lucas took a dive off the deep end and gave passionate love between males and females the worst possible rap. Anybody else notice this? As of the second Star Wars trilogy, it is okay for Jedi knights to lie, cheat, steal and murder. They cannot, however, love, because love makes you angry. In Lucas' universe, lying, cheating, stealing and murdering can apparently all be done calmly, rationally and with a sound heart, but love, especially loving your mother, only leads to trouble.

If I'm going to spend time in a fantasy universe, give me Pullman's take on the power of love any day.

The power of love, however, is not simple in this universe. Love has a very dark side. Love can be manipulated and used. It is the first evil we see in the books. It is what Mrs. Coulter does.

The children who look at Mrs. Coulter are not afraid; they are in love. They do what she says not because she threatens them but because she makes them love her. Love brings trust, and that trust is betrayed. Even Lyra falls in love with her, until Mrs. Coulter shows Lyra the violence that underlies the facade of love.

What I find interesting about that scene is that it is not Lyra or Mrs. Coulter involved directly in the attack—it is the dæmons. The golden monkey attacks Pantalaimon.

Had Lyra been hit herself, she might have followed a standard pattern for abuse victims. She might have excused the incident, decided it was her fault and become determined not to repeat the mistake. But the attack was made on the being Lyra most loved, and that completely changed her attitude toward Mrs. Coulter. Lyra will not love the one who attacks Pantalaimon, and so her travels and adventures begin again. Here is another way in which Pullman explores the true and complex implications of the bond between humans and dæmons.

Even more than love, the trope of the Boy Warrior undergoes its greatest transformation in Pullman's hands.

There are more Boy Warriors in fantasy literature than there are Telepathic Girls. Boys fifteen years old and younger are constantly being thrust into manhood by killing an enemy. Within the world of the novel, this is generally considered a right and proper, even vitally necessary, part of growing up. How else can the Boy Warrior become the Boy King, free his friends, save the world or otherwise achieve his quest? There's a bad guy in the way, he's got to die and the hero's got to do it—how else can he truly be the hero?

What you seldom see these novels exploring is the damage that becoming a killer does to the human psyche, especially when that human being is still a child.

It's actually extremely hard to get a human being to kill another human being. To make a modern soldier, you must take the young person away from all their friends and family, subject them to extremely harsh physical and psychological conditions and forge a bond of love between them and their immediate colleagues. When they kill, they are killing to protect these new loved ones. You must also dehumanize the enemy in every way possible. You cannot allow the soldier to truly believe that the person at the other end of the gun is a fellow human or they will hesitate to take that enemy life.

Will Parry at first kills unintentionally. While an accident breaks his enemy's neck, it is profoundly disturbing. To realize that not only must he kill, but that he is capable of killing shakes his image of self and soul profoundly and repeatedly. He tries again and again to find an adult to take the burden of this knowledge from him. He wants his father or his mother to protect him from himself and what he's done. But he does not have them, and so he must shut off feeling of what he's done, or go insane. In shutting off a part of his human feeling, he becomes cold and ferocious. Rather than a natural, necessary, sanitary progression to adulthood and heroism, it is damage to self and psyche that make Will into a warrior. What happens to Will is loss and diminishment, not growth and gain.

Boy Warriors are also commonly orphans, either physically or emotionally. In order to be a true hero, it seems the character's family must be dead or evil. The path to heroism starts with the slaughter of the home village, for example, or the understanding that one's royal father is a miserable tyrant. This aloneness is frequently used to make the hero into something more noble and make him a more suitable object of love for the heroine. Will's aloneness, on the other hand, is portrayed as profoundly tragic. It is what frightens him at night and breaks his heart during the day. He wishes bitterly that it were not part of his life. It leaves him nothing but tired and frightened, and because Pullman returns to these feelings repeatedly we are made to understand there is nothing noble in Will's suffering. Like his wounded hand, it is only another thing he must endure.

Interestingly, Pullman does not do any examination of this kind with Lyra. In Lyra, he creates the emotional orphan. Lyra's parents are both evil of one sort or another, and she is emotionally abandoned and physically abused by them both. But where Will's aloneness is examined in excruciating detail, Lyra's bewilderment and detachment are treated perfunctorily. Lyra is given the ability to hate in a straightforward and uncomplicated fashion, even when it comes to her own parents, and yet at no time does this intense ability and willingness to hate interfere with her ability to love. Lyra's heart goes out instantly to a whole host of characters, from Iorek to Lee Scoresby, to Serafina, to Will.

This is a dichotomy I find problematic. Why is Pullman so willing and able to explore what the loss of family does to the boy in his story, but not the girl? Lyra's emotional suffering is done at a remove. Where we see her most full of self-doubt is in *The Subtle Knife*; and there we see it from Will's point of view, not Lyra's. She is spiritually ferocious and, unlike Will, undamaged by her ferocity.

Lyra also never kills anyone.

I'm not sure I understand this choice. Lyra wishes to kill her enemies numerous times but never quite gets around to it; Will, who just wants to go home, kills repeatedly. In his rejection and rework of cliché, Pullman commits one of the biggest—the male warrior and the female instigator. Given that this is an exact echo of the way Lord Asriel and Mrs. Coulter work, I can't see it as inadvertent. It is part and parcel with one of the biggest weakness of the trilogy. In his fearless deconstruction of fantasy trope, Pullman does not employ one of the standard tools of the fantasy author, and without it, the story is much weaker and more confusing than it would be otherwise.

Pullman never explains Lyra.

Yes, we get the story of her birth, but she is never explained. Why can she and no one else read the alethiometer? Why do people fall in love with her so fiercely? Is that something she inherited from her mother? If it's genetic, where did her mother get it from?

Which leads to a whole host of questions, all of which show that in failing to truly explain Lyra, Pullman also never adequately explains the magic of his universe, and here is where the story begins to crack.

Pullman does not mind taking time out of the story as an omniscient narrator to explain things. He has his characters ruminate for long periods on the fundamental underpinnings of nature. In fact, Pullman spends pages and pages explaining the nature of his universe, exploring and deconstructing the underpinnings of Christian theology and any reason to believe in any form of organized religion whatsoever. For all this epic exploring and explaining, he does not take a moment to perform one of the most basic tasks of successful fantasy literature.

Now, look, I'm not a big fan of magic "systems." I regard Dungeons & Dragons as one of the worst things to ever happen to fantasy literature. Magic does not follow the laws of math and physics and it should not be made to because this makes magic small and unmiraculous, if not downright comic. Where magic follows rules, those rules are traditionally closer to the rules of diplomacy and courtesy than the scientific law. Magic, in my opinion, was originally and should remain big, mysterious and risky.

But it should also make *some kind* of sense within the story. If the little old man under the rock with whom the hero's shared his lunch grants him three wishes, the old man should not show up in Book Two with a fourth wish without a really good reason. Equally, the hero should not suddenly be able to pass out wishes on his own. If elves have magic and humans don't at the beginning of a story, a human with magic should not appear without exploration and explanation. To do so violates the primary rule of fantastic and speculative storytelling. You must, must, *must* be internally consistent.

Pullman is not. He creates two incredibly powerful beings, Lord Asriel and Mrs. Coulter. He keeps increasing their power in each of the books, and he does not once explain who these two are or how they came to be so powerful and there is no sense given of any of their limits. In a story about the non-existence of God, these two are deus ex machinas. They can do anything the author needs them to do whenever he needs them to do it. They do not make any sense at all and they fit nowhere. If they were just other beings tossed into the war for the enlarging effect of the story, I wouldn't have a problem, but these are major actors and as such they create a tremendous weakness in the foundation of the story.

Thus Lyra at bottom remains a partially completed character. She is what she is because the author needs her to get his message across, not because she has arisen naturally from the world of the story. How can we understand her if we can't understand Mrs. Coulter and Asriel?

Pullman makes the same mistake with the figure of John Parry, who becomes a magician with power of greater strength and range than any of the witches we meet, even when they are acting together. He gains them, as near as we can tell, through dint of study and having a hole drilled in his head. Why is he able to gain these powers? We don't really know. Could anybody who was willing to have a hole drilled in their head gain these powers? Again, we don't know. And, most importantly for the storytelling, what are the extent and nature of his powers? We never find out. Parry can do exactly what he has to, and never fails to do anything required. He, at least, does run out of strength eventually, which never happens to Asriel and Coulter.

But even this is not the most important missing explanation. At the denouement, we have no explanation at all why it is Will and Lyra's love in particular that saves the universe. Yes, they're special. We get that. But if, as Pullman seems to be saying, every act of passionate love is an affirmation of independence and creation in this universe, why is Theirs so essentially different it can heal evil? Especially when it can't and doesn't last?

Left to itself as it is, the ability of Will and Lyra to save all seems to come down to destiny, which is extremely jarring because one of the main thrusts of the story is that pre-destination is a bad and artificial thing, a thing created by an overly controlling angel with delusions of grandeur and abetted by a cruel and mindless Church.

The power of destiny is the last major fantasy trope that Pullman takes on, and, unfortunately, the one he seems to do the least well by. Over and over he explains how pre-ordination is connected with the forces that want to promote mindless obedience. And yet, without the fundamental explanations of their parents and their powers, Will and Lyra become creatures of destiny. If he's making a point about how even God screws up when it comes to trying to organize what humans will and won't do and how it will result, that's fine, but because he's been so careful to explain every other metaphysical aspect of Dust and angels, why doesn't he explain this?

In the end, for all his attempts to break down trope, archetype and cliché, Pullman's ambitious work falls to the greatest and the worst of them: the need to serve his own message no matter what. So intent is Pullman on getting his message of the ultimate positive nature of love, life and the natural universe across, he fails to see that the message is warping the weave of the story, and in some places warping it so badly that all you can see is the message. The emotional power and range that are inherent to fiction are lost, and there's nothing left but polemic.

Pullman is far from being the first fantasy author to fall under the burden of message, nor is he anywhere near the worst, but in this case it is a particular shame. What he does well, he does very well indeed. There is so much in His Dark Materials that is rich, original and fear-less it shines in a genre overloaded with the drab and the everyday. The reworking and rearranging of so many of the most tired and overworked tropes is to be cheered and enjoyed. Perhaps, however, if Pullman had not tried to break apart so much in one story, the cracks would not show so badly when he came to put it back together again.

Sarah Zettel was born in Sacramento, CA. Shortly after this she embarked on a wide and varied reading career from ten cities, four states and two countries. This combined to give her a wide and varied range of opinions, some of which are included in this book, and eventually settled her in the life of a science fiction and fantasy author. She is currently at work on her twelfth novel. Sarah lives in Michigan with her husband Tim, son Alexander and cat, Buffy the Vermin Slayer.

ROBERT A. METZGER

Philip Pullman, Research Scientist

We take such comfort from labels.

Before me are the volumes that make up Philip Pullman's His Dark Materials trilogy. Picking them up and thumbing through, I can't help but catch key words and phrases, those that should help me label just what these books are all about: dæmons, angels, a subtle knife, armored bears, Gobblers and witches.

Witches.

Even a quick scan clues me in that these aren't twenty-first-century witches, those who live in Manhattan, practice the art of aromatherapy and make the pilgrimage to upstate New York in the comfort of their Land Rovers during the summer solstice, where upon arrival they'll run about naked in an apple orchard as they feel the mud squish between their toes. Not Pullman's witches—these are of the pine branch-riding variety who chop up cliff ghasts.

Can there be any doubt as to what sort of books I have before me? I'm looking at fantasy here. And if any doubt at all remained, the back cover of my edition of *The Golden Compass* should put that to rest, proclaiming that what I hold in my hand is a "modern fantasy classic."

Okay.

The label has been applied—but not just to the books.

A label has also been applied to me—the reader of these books. Who am I? What am I? You see me walking through the bookstore with Pullman's His Dark Materials tucked beneath my arm and you think here is someone who appreciates fantasy at its finest—the fantastic mixed with overtones of literature.

That would be true.

But you might be surprised as to what else I am. I'm also a scientist and a science fiction writer. Are there a few eyebrows being raised? Does that not quite fit into your world view of a fantasy reader? Not so sure how to label me? Do scientists read "modern fantasy classics"? Can a science fiction writer's interest be held through 1300 pages of a "modern fantasy classic"?

Perhaps I'm not the sort of scientist and science fiction writer that the label generator in your head has conjured up. Afraid not—I'm probably dead-on. I've spent decades in research labs and universities mucking around with hulking stainless steel vacuum vessels, power supplies pumping out enough juice to carbonize a wayward limb, toxic chemicals that could peel flesh to the bone—and all of this in the quest of inserting atoms of specific flavors into just the right atomic locations of a growing crystalline lattice. I was a scientist from a tender age. What comes to mind when you think of the high school senior who is given an award at graduation for being the best science student in a class of 1,200 kids? That was me.

I'm sure it's not a pretty picture.

I can imagine the picture in your head—pocket protector bristling with pens, tweezers, miniature screwdrivers and little doodads with mirrors and claws. There are probably Coke bottle-thick lenses inserted in the black plastic-framed glasses slipping down a nose. And I have no doubt that this individual's pants legs are short by an inch or two so as to show an ample swatch of sock about the ankle, and hair style oscillates between that of a flattop buzz or an Einstein comb-free bush.

Oh, yes.

I know what you're thinking. And while I'd like to think that I've acquired enough of the social graces to pass in public as an insurance salesman or even a high school history teacher, I will admit that in times past I may have sported a few of the stereotypical science-geek traits.

And then add insult to injury.

I write science fiction, and not just any old science fiction, but that at the far end of the science fiction spectrum: hard sf, the type where one might expect the neutron stars and warp drives in the tales to have more personality than the characters, the type where key plot developments turn on the hero's ability to recite mathematical constants to better than a hundred significant digits.

So what is a science/sf geek doing reading His Dark Materials?

It's because I figured out a few things while toiling away in the world of science.

Science is not about equations.

Science is not about big machines and the stink of ozone.

Science is not about chemical-stained lab coats.

And science is not about socially inept folks whose only quality relationships revolve around their computers or lab animals.

No.

Science is Magic. Science is a Quest. Science is a human endeavor.

And Philip Pullman not only understands this, but features it as a central theme. I would even go so far as to say that Philip Pullman is not a writer at all, but a most remarkable research scientist who has so eloquently detailed his grand experiment in a text titled His Dark Materials.

Now be careful here.

Don't start labeling things again. I'm not talking about the *engineering* that you find in His Dark Materials, of which there is plenty. Consider the machine that Lyra discovers at the Oblation's Board's secret lab in the far northern lands of Svalbard—the one used for separating child from dæmon. This contraption is based on Maystadt's anbaric scalpel and further refined by Lord Asriel's discoveries about the unique properties of manganese and titanium alloys when sharpened to atomic perfection—it is a dæmon-cleaving guillotine. However, none of that is science.

That's engineering.

Give a few million monkeys a few billion years and they would probably stumble upon the technique of constructing the dæmon-cleaving blade.

Pullman doesn't do engineering. He does science, cutting right to the magic of it. The magic of science is that a simple concept, one that at first glance might seem almost trivial, actually has far ranging and often unimaginable consequences. Science is an attitude about how to look at the world, an attitude that transforms the mundane into the magical. A single elegant and well-thought-out experiment has more magic to it than a boat-load of troll-laden fantasy sagas. And Pullman understands this.

Consider Sir Isaac Newton when he got clobbered by that apple.

You've all heard about that. But do you know what it means, where the magic was in that moment? When that apple struck Newton on the noggin, an answer was not revealed to him. That is one of the great misconceptions of how science works. *Scientists are not in the business of seeking answers.*

Answers are a dime a dozen.

What makes a scientist is the *questions* they ask. Ask the right question and that is when the magic happens. When Newton was bonked by the apple, he asked himself a question—if some unknown force had acted on that apple, pulling it down toward the Earth (where he just happened to be in the way), wouldn't that force act on *everything* else, not just an apple?

That was *the* question.

And does that question lead to another, thought Newton.

After all, there is nothing special about apples. So if this mysterious force acts on apples, then it should act on everything—Newton himself, the moon above and even the distant planets. And if the gravity of the Earth acted to pull that apple down, and since he had already drawn the conclusion that there was no fundamental difference between apples and planets with regard to this force, then wouldn't it follow that the gravity generated by an apple would also act to pull the Earth up toward it?

Oh yes. This is called the *eureka* moment—the essence of scientific magic.

Gravity acts on everything.

Asking the question of why the apple fell *down* led to understanding how the entire universe is put together, allowed us centuries later to fly men to the moon, keep airplanes from dropping from the sky and guaranteed an endless supply of microwave popcorn. It has created the very world in which you live.

If that is not magic, then I don't know what is.

Ask the right question and a new world is revealed.

And this is what Pullman has done.

The manganese-titanium blade is an engineering device used to separate child from dæmon. But the science, the magic of it, goes so much further. If that guillotine can sever the bond between child and dæmon, then what else can it cut, just what is it that is actually being cut when this mysterious alloy is sharpened to atomic perfection?

Pullman asks *the* question, just like any good research scientist would.

We first encounter that manganese-titanium alloy in *The Golden Compass*, but Pullman does not let it fade away—it's not just a piece of fictionally induced hardware to further a plotline. The razor edge of that guillotine is not simply an item to be found in a run-of-the-mill fantasy—not just another piece of fantasy hardware like a potion brewed of toadstools and unicorn blood or a talisman infused with the power of the ancient ones.

No, it's science.

Pullman asks, if that alloy can cut away dæmons, then just what is it that is being cut? Like any good scientist Pullman needs to run a few experiments, those that will help guide him in his quest of asking the right questions, the answers to which will allow him to build a self-consistent, rational world.

Enter *The Subtle Knife.*

While the knife can cut through anything in the macroscopic world, like the armor of a bear or the fingers of Will Parry, it cuts much deeper, much finer, far beyond the macroscopic world of Oxford and hydrogen-filled dirigibles. In a work of science fiction, one might expect such a blade to operate in the realm of quantum mechanics, where that perfect edge could sever the bonds between atoms. Science fiction is full of such wonderful blades—I in fact invented one just like it out of pure carbon to create a diamond blade whose edge would slice atomic bonds in my first hard sf novel *Quad World* that was published back in 1991. But Pullman goes far beyond the world of quantum mechanics.

Not so much *beyond*, but *deeper.*

Not interested in something as massive as individual atoms and the bonds that bind them, Pullman finds something more fundamental to slice away at—space-time—the very fabric of reality, a region that physicists are only now beginning to explore using the theoretical tools of string theory and quantum loop gravity. These theorists operate in realms a billion-billion-billion times smaller than the size of a single atom where the underlying construction of the universe is no longer smooth and featureless, but a boiling froth of what they call Planck-foam—a place where reality itself is an explosion of particles and wormholes, those wormholes magically connecting different regions of space-time by routes outside the normal geometry of this universe's space-time.

That's the domain where Pullman's subtle knife operates.

He asked this question: if a perfect blade constructed of titanium and manganese could shred the fabric of space-time in order to remove a dæmon from a child, then shouldn't it also be able to cut away at space-time for other purposes?

And that of course is just what Will Parry's subtle knife does, slicing openings in space-time itself, creating gateways to parallel worlds—the sort of parallel universes that physicists have been theorizing about for decades, each world a possibility generated by the collapse of a single quantum event.

Infinite quantum events.

Infinite parallel worlds.

And Pullman has figured out how to move between these worlds.

The subtle knife is not just another gizmo to push along a fantasy plot. It is a scientific necessity in a universe where a soul-cleaving blade exists. If you can manipulate space-time to cut away a soul, then you can also use it to slice through higher dimensions, penetrating the fabric of space-time and open portals to parallel universes.

That is the essence of science.

The magic is in the wonder and consequences of asking the right question. But Pullman goes much deeper than this. Scientists have much more than a single tool in their toolbox—they have the ability to ask the right question and to then follow the consequences of that answer to their absolute limits.

Scientists also operate under a set of *beliefs*.

On the surface this might sound like a very unscientific thing. Some will try to portray science as a sledgehammer to shatter beliefs, as a method used to quantify and prove things and then to discount and ignore everything that cannot be quantified with a formula.

No.

Nowhere is the concept of belief more apparent than with Albert Einstein. When he examined quantum mechanics, where nothing is absolute, where everything is described in terms of probabilities and potentials, with nothing fixed, he rejected it. Quantum mechanics is used to describe how the world on the atomic scale operates. An understanding of quantum mechanics opened the way for such things that run the gamut from nuclear weapons to integrated circuits. It works. It explains things.

Einstein understood the usefulness of quantum mechanics.

But he did not *believe* that it was the true description of how the world actually operated. He could not prove it to be inadequate, but *believed* it to be inadequate. In what may be his most famous quote, Einstein said that *"God does not play dice,"* meaning that the probabilistic nature of quantum mechanics was simply wrong. It was his belief that if he could ask the right question, a deeper level of understanding would be revealed to him, exposing an underlying principle that would explain how the universe worked, a generalized principle that would describe not only how the gravitational fields of black holes warp space, but how individual atoms interact. And what would be revealed to him would not be a universe of probabilities and quantum spookiness, but a place that reflected the beauty of its Creator.

Einstein believed in a rational universe created by a rational Creator. Einstein believed in cause and effect, where there exists an understandable relationship between an atom in your fingertip and a curl of plasma being ejected from the sun.

All connected. All understandable.

That is what scientists strive for—to ask the questions that will uncover those fundamental principles that govern the universe. That's magic. Einstein spent the last thirty years of his life searching for what is now called the Theory of Everything and never did find it. In the half century since his death, physicists continue to search for ways to unify what appear to be such different forces as those of gravity, electromagnetism and nuclear. Scientists operate from a belief that the world is understandable, that cause and effect always exist and that there is a connection between things. The leading contender for such a unifying theory is called string theory, one that relies on a universe constructed out of eleven dimensions (seven more than we can experience with our senses); many theoretical physicists are attracted to it for no practical reason—but because the underlying math used in the theory is described by many to be so *beautiful* and *elegant*, it must hold some fundamental truth.

That is the exact mindset that Pullman operates under when constructing his fictional worlds. He has the belief of a scientist, looking for a unifying principle, something *beautiful* and *elegant* to explain how his fictional worlds operate, how what appear to be a nearly infinite number of observations are actually all manifestations of a single underlying principle.

How does Pullman pull that off?

He invents Dust.

At the start of His Dark Materials, hints are given as to the nature of Dust—a mysterious material that few even suspect exists; fewer still can even make a guess as to what it is. It appears to be a substance separate from man but may have some connection to man. We learn soon enough that Dust seems to have an affinity to adults, while not to children.

That is our first big clue as to the true nature of Dust—the first scientific question asked in order to gain further insight into its true nature. If Dust behaves differently around children and adults, then doesn't that say something about the differences between children and adults?

Yes.

Children are not simply miniature adults. Children are on a journey to not only find their way and place into the world, but to find their way to themselves. Again Pullman offers up another piece of scientific evidence to the puzzle. The dæmons of children are not fixed, but continually shift in form, which is a reflection of the child's attitudes and temperament. Only when adulthood has been reached do the dæmon forms settle, as humans understand just what they are.

To know yourself.

To be conscious of yourself.

And that of course is the key. We begin to realize this as we read through His Dark Materials; we start to think that perhaps we are finally getting a handle on Dust. Perhaps it is attracted to the self-aware? But certainly it must be more than just some exotic material that clings to conscious beings like oppositely charged particles. Never forget that Pullman has constructed a rational, scientifically principled universe.

How does Lyra's alethiometer possibly work? If this were simply a troll-laden fantasy full of enchanted swords and flapping dragons, the alethiometer would most likely be just one more enchanted gizmo. But of course Pullman does not operate like that—a writer with the soul of a research scientist would never rely on such a crutch to hold a story together.

The alethiometer sees all—not just the physical aspects of the world where an armored bear is lurking, or a witch hiding, but knows what is going on inside their heads, in their souls; it reveals to Lyra their thoughts and desires. But it does even more. It has access to *every* world.

How?

Think about Pullman's perspective, the perspective of a scientist. Systems are rational, understandable and *connected*. If the alethiometer can tell Lyra and Will about Will's father in another world, then there must be a direct connection between those worlds, a medium through which this information is being channeled.

Dust, of course.

The alethiometer is a type of Dust radio, able with the operator to isolate the infinite signals pouring between countless worlds in order to find the answer to any question. More insight into Dust.

But of course there is much more to learn.

And for the next level of understanding Pullman doesn't use a witch, a fairy, a magic amulet or ancient scroll. He gives us a scientist—Mary Malone. And what a scientist. As a scientist myself, and knowing the backgrounds of hundreds of scientists, I can tell you that most of us follow a pretty similar path in quest of our lab coats. Our science ways show at an early age. We enjoy math, we take things apart to see how they work and we are the annoying children who pester adults with such non-trivial questions such as why is the sky blue, how do light bulbs work and why can't I breathe underwater? From there we move on to university, taking the prescribed undergraduate curriculum to give us the tools of science: the physics, math, chemistry and engineering to understand the mechanics of how the world works. And from there we move on to graduate school where we are supposed to use these tools to light up a bit of the dark, to ask a few questions of our own and find out something new, to make a few more connections that in turn give all of us a better understanding of the world.

But Pullman won't settle for that.

Remember that for Pullman science is a magnificent thing, a thing of beauty, a belief in and of itself. So Mary Malone does not take the standard route. Before giving herself to science, she'd first given herself to something else—God.

Now I know that His Dark Materials has raised quite a stir of controversy about Pullman's view of the Church—that some believe this is a tale in which the heroes do nothing less than destroy a corrupt and uncaring God. I'm no theologian and am not equipped to venture into that argument.

But I am a scientist.

And I was raised a Catholic.

So I think I can see a bit into Mary Malone. I don't believe that her desertion of the Church for science was an act of her turning her back on her beliefs. Nothing of the sort. Mary believes in the wonder of the universe, in the beauty of it, a place so magnificent that she is certain that its Creator wants us to experience it as fully as our consciousness will allow.

Mary makes a very definite distinction between the Church and the Creator.

Her beliefs cannot be held within the limited confines of the Church.

The universe is simply too magnificent and wonderful to not explore.

So she did not abandon her beliefs, but let them grow beyond the confines of the Church. And as part of that journey she discovered Dust, and with the help of Lyra discovered the key insight about Dust. It is not an inert substance that connects all conscious beings—it is conscious itself.

Another layer revealed.

If we've been paying attention to the previous one thousand plus pages that bring us to the point of Mary conversing with Dust, we should suspect that Dust is more than just another player in a large cast of characters. Again, if you realize that Pullman is constructing His Dark Materials with the eye of a research scientist, you need to consider that Dust is not some independent phenomenon, not even a cog in a giant machine—but something that keeps all the cogs smoothly meshing, connected to everything around it, both *impacting* the world and the people in it, as well as being *impacted by* the world and the characters in it.

Impacted is probably too subtle a word to describe the relationship between conscious entities and Dust. As Lyra discovers during her journey through the world of the dead, Dust is created by self-aware individuals. It is a finite resource, a thing that can be spread too far and wide and must be continually replenished.

To make certain that we understand this point, Pullman again turns to Mary Malone to explain it to us through her investigation of the Mulefa. With Mary's invention of the amber spyglass that allows her to see Dust, she is able to figure out the ecology of the Mulefa's world, to understand the connections between things that give her the insight into just how the world works. And by understanding how that single world works, it leads her, Lyra and Will to understand how all the worlds work.

The Mulefa's ecology is incredibly simple (much simpler than any actual ecology—Pullman, apparently not wanting to embellish or complicate at this point, wanted to make sure in no uncertain terms that we get *his* point). The Mulefa's world operates with three basic elements: the Mulefa, the trees and Dust. The Mulefa, being conscious beings, generate Dust. The Dust in turn fertilizes the flowers in the trees, ensuring that they will flourish. The trees in turn produce the nuts which supply so much to the Mulefa, not the least of which are their use as wheels which evolution has designed to mesh perfectly with Mulefa anatomy. Through the Mulefa's act of using the nuts as wheels, the nuts experience constant pounding which eventually cracks them, revealing the seeds within— which the Mulefa plant in order to propagate the forests.

This is a circle complete through an incredibly simply ecology—one that's too simple for its own good. Such single-path ecologies are highly susceptible to collapse since it only takes the failure of a single element to cause the entire system to come crashing down. This is just what is happens since the pathways of the Dust have been perturbed; they no longer float down to the trees, but are being pulled out of the Mulefa's world and into other worlds through the many portals that have been opened by the subtle knife. By the time Mary arrives, the process has radically accelerated as a result of Lord Asriel's experiments that have led to the merging of so many worlds.

Of course the Dust is aware of all this—that is why it sent Mary Malone into the Mulefa's world in the first place, not only for her to discover the true nature of the world, but to find Lyra and Will so she could act as the catalyst to push them through the adolescent barrier to adulthood—or as is pointed out so many times in the books, Mary will take on the role of the serpent to Lyra's Eve.

Knowledge of self expels one from the Garden of Eden.

And science is the instrument that Pullman uses to pull the trigger.

Or so it would seem on the surface.

But it is of critical importance to recall that it is not some science fact, some scientific formula or some uncovered scientific principle that propels Lyra from childhood to adulthood and subsequently leads her and Will to not only repairing the damage done by the Church and the subtle knife, but to rescuing the soul of every person who has ever died.

No, Mary simply recounts to Lyra a tale from her own adolescence—the story of marzipan, how that sweet taste, representative of all the wonder in the universe, revealed to her the infinite possibilities in the world. It was something so human, so full of wonder, something so essentially human—the memory and feelings of love. And it is a scientist who brings this message, because this is what scientists understand, what they strive for, the beliefs that drive them in seeking the magic in the universe.

That's it—the full arc of His Dark Materials completed.

Science is a most human endeavor and as such is infused with all things human, the most essential of which, the most powerful, is love. Can there be any doubt that Pullman is a research scientist extraordinaire?

Robert A. Metzger is a research scientist and a science fiction and science writer. His research focuses on the technique of Molecular Beam Epitaxy, used to grow epitaxial films for high-speed electronics applications. His short fiction has appeared in most major sf magazines including: Asimov's, Fantasy & Science Fiction, *and* SF Age, *while his 2002 novel* Picoverse *was a Nebula finalist and his most recent novel,* Cusp, *was released by Ace in 2005. His science writing has appeared in* Wired *and* Analog, *and he is a contributing editor to the Science Fiction Writers of American Bulletin.*

ARTHUR B. MARKMAN

Science, Technology and the Danger of Dæmons

I read Pullman's His Dark Materials trilogy aloud to one of my sons when he was about nine. Needless to say, he loved it. When I told him that I was going to write an essay about the books, he asked me to say that the dæmons in Lyra's world are really the people's consciences. I am a cognitive psychologist who studies the way people think, and so his suggestion was not totally off-base—though it also was not exactly what I wanted to write about.

What really interests me about the books is Pullman's cautionary view of the pursuit of knowledge and the advance of technology. He does not display any particular love of academics with their elite institutions. He is particularly skeptical of technological advances arising from this knowledge, which can lead to disastrous outcomes both intended and unintended.

So, at first, it seemed that I would have to disappoint my son and focus on the evils wrought by scholars and the release of Specters by the subtle knife rather than examining how Pantalaimon is a physical manifestation of Lyra's inner world.

And yet, perhaps I don't, because there is an analogy of the relationship between conscience and mind on the one hand and between technology and the world on the other. The lessons that psychologists are learning about the structure of the mind are similar to Pullman's cautionary tale about the potential pitfalls of knowledge and technology.

To draw this analogy, we have to start by spending some time thinking about theories about the way the mind works. Then we'll return to science, academics and technology.

While we all have the experience of consciousness, consciousness is a bit of a puzzle. We know from our own experiences that we are self-aware, conscious of ourselves and the world around us—we experience emotions, colors and sounds, and make mental decisions that drive our actions. And while there are many theories of consciousness, there is no undisputed science of consciousness. If your computer woke up tomorrow and announced that it was conscious (and demanded its rights under the constitution), we'd have virtually no way of knowing whether it was really conscious or just pretending to be conscious (for example by a practical-joking virus). Our experience of consciousness is not a reliable guide to how consciousness really works.

We experience consciousness in what the philosopher Dan Dennett calls the Cartesian Theater. We have a coherent experience of the world around us as if we are watching a movie consisting of visual images, accompanying sounds, tastes, smells and feelings. It comes with an internal monologue that speaks our inner thoughts. We can even have imagined dialogs with ourselves in which thoughts pop out at us as if something inside is answering back to our questions.

But our experience of consciousness is a poor guide to truly understanding it. If our conscious experiences really were projected into some kind of Cartesian Theater, someone or something would have to be in there to watch the images, smell the smells, feel the feelings and speak the thoughts. If your goal is to explain how thinking works, then resorting to a ghost-in-the-machine like this (what philosophers have called the *homunculus*) does not solve any problems, because eventually you would need a theory of the psychology of the homunculus. If you are a writer, however, you can make this homunculus a physical being, and create a world in which it lives outside and actually does converse with the rest of the person. So, Pantalaimon can be Lyra's homunculus. When people in Lyra's world are separated from their dæmon, they act as though there is no longer anyone viewing their Cartesian Theater (of course, this begs the question of who Patalaimon's homunculus is).

The compelling vision of the homunculus is a legacy of the seventeenth-century philosopher and mathematician Rene Descartes. One of his central contributions to philosophy of mind was the notion of *dualism*. He believed that the mind—that stuff that provides us with our self-awareness and ability to think—is separate from our brains—that physical stuff that controls our physical body. Very few psychologists or philosophers are true dualists any more, because of the logical and empirical problems associated with dualism. But the belief persists in a separation of mind and brain—our individual feeling that one has a brain, rather than that one is part of a brain. And this loose dualism is very much part of psychological thinking to this day.

Even though we acknowledge that the brain produces our thoughts, most psychologists typically assume that thinking is quite separate from perceiving the world and acting on it. The idea is that our eyes, ears and body send some information to our brain, which acts as a kind of information processing computer that does some fancy calculation, thinks some nifty thoughts and then tells our body how to move, where to go and what to do next. Much of the research on thinking that has been done for the past fifty years has made this assumption (at least implicitly).

More recently, however, psychologists have begun to realize that the distinction between thinking and action is much less clear than we've assumed. For example, children do not begin to show fear of heights until they begin to move around the world themselves. It is not that they cannot see depth, they can do that very early. It is just that they don't relate the perception of depth with the idea of falling. Only when kids begin to connect their visual experiences to their motor actions moving through the world do they begin to actively try to keep themselves from crawling off a high surface.

In another example, people's attitudes are more positive when they are making a smiling face than when they are making a frowning face. To demonstrate this phenomenon without telling people to smile or frown, clever psychologists had people give their attitude toward a variety of objects while either holding a pen sideways in their teeth (which causes the person's lips to smile) or holding the end of a pen in their teeth (which causes the person's lips to frown). People expressed more positive attitudes when they were making a smiling face than when they were making a frowning face, even though they did not (consciously) realize the face they were making. Something about the connection between these smiling and frowning movements was affecting the way people processed information in order to express attitudes. Movement drove thinking rather than the other way around.

This recognition that thinking is intimately connected with the way people perceive the world and move through it is called *embodied cognition*. It reflects that the central purpose of thinking is to control a body moving in space. Yes, humans are capable of amazing abstract thought, but even when we try to think abstractly it helps to form a specific image of the abstract concept we are trying to reason about.

So, how does this relate to the discussion of technology in the Pullman trilogy? Just as our thinking is informed by our movement through the world and our perception of the world, so our technological thinking must be informed by the outside world that will be affected by this technological thinking. Just as the mind is deeply interconnected to the systems that allow us to perceive and act on the world, so too are many facets of the world deeply interconnected. Of course, technological thinking in the academic world is often separated from the world in which information is going to be used, to the detriment of academic study and to those who reap the fruits of this work.

Furthermore, even people who devote their lives to the study of a particular topic can be blind to the degree to which the elements of their domain of expertise are deeply interconnected. As we have seen, scientific psychology has worked with a computational view of mind that has not recognized how deeply the information people process is affected by the way they perceive and act on the world. Science can get locked into a particular view of the world that makes it difficult to recognize deep relationships among facets of the world. This narrow perspective makes the emergence of unintended consequences that much more likely.

Now we are ready to return to technology in the trilogy. At first glance, Lyra's Oxford seems very different from our own world (as seen in Will's Oxford). For one thing, Lyra's Oxford seems to be more technologically similar to nineteenth-century England than to twenty-first-century England. This slower pace of development strikes me as quite likely, given that knowledge in Lyra's Oxford appears to be more tightly controlled by a small group of people than in Will's Oxford. The scholars at Jordan College do not disseminate information widely. There does not seem to be a high level of compulsory education for the common people. Science is the province of the wealthy rather than being a vocation available to anyone who shows interest. In Lyra's Oxford, Mary Malone would never have been able to enter the ranks of the scientists.

But our world is not that much better than Lyra's. For one, knowledge is quite centralized in our world. While it is true that nearly anyone in our world can obtain an education and rise into the ranks of the elite who pursue knowledge, few people do. Most of us are content to rely on the knowledge of experts. We have to be, of course. Nobody can be an expert in everything. (And this is also true for areas of expertise that need not be considered elite. Most of us cannot fix an air conditioner. It is not just that we would prefer not to and so we hire someone else to do it; we couldn't do it even if we had to.)

This means that the belief that people in modern society are knowledgeable is an illusion based on the easy availability of expert opinions on television, in the newspaper and on the Web. Few of us have the ability to evaluate the information we are given by experts. Conversations around the water cooler at work about global warming, economic decay and politics often involve passing around expert analysis and opinions that were gleaned from the media rather than derived by the speaker.

Thus, knowledge in our society is becoming dangerously analogous to a brain that is not connected to the systems that perceive and act on the world. Our day-to-day use of knowledge in contexts like politics is not practical knowledge. It is not the sort of knowledge that politicians must use to solve difficult problems. Instead, it is knowledge that is designed for persuasion.

So while, unlike in Lyra's world, our scientists share information freely, nevertheless the highly specialized nature of scientific research makes true dissemination of information quite narrow.

But control of information is even stronger in Lyra's Oxford, where knowledge is clearly the province of the elite. The dangers of elite science are made repeatedly by Pullman, perhaps most strikingly by the abuses of the scientists at Bolvangar. The researchers there developed the silver guillotine that could be used to sever the connection between a person and his or her dæmon. This technology was used brutally and without regard for the effect that it had on the lives of the people who were treated with it. At Bolvangar, it was used to create a class of servants who would assist with the children who were being kept as research subjects without influencing the scientific studies being done. This misuse of science is reminiscent of the horrible studies carried out on humans during the Nazi regime during World War II, in which helpless people were subjected to studies without regard to the potential dangers of this research to the participants.

How does the segregation of knowledge in an elite class contribute to this misuse of technology? Expanding the limits of knowledge always has ethical ramifications. Sometimes new knowledge threatens to overturn strong cultural belief systems, as when knowledge about the solar system revealed that the sun rather than the earth was at the center. Other times, new knowledge creates ethical dilemmas, such as the current debates about whether we should permit cloning of human beings.

Unlike scientific problems, where we can look to the world for answers, ethical problems do not have objective solutions. In our world we tend to seek solutions to ethical problems that maximize the benefits of science to the most people, while minimizing the risks. However, our society also has certain deeply held cultural and religious beliefs that influence the solution of ethical problems. A critical part of the process of deciding how to deal with ethical problems is broad discussion. This discussion requires that scientists communicate with the nonscientific community, to make clear the potential benefits of the acquisition of new knowledge in an area. In our world, issues like stem cell research and human cloning are debated by society as a whole.

Lyra's world did not take the dissemination of scientific information as a priority. Indeed, the Church did not permit open discussion of scientific concepts. Lord Asriel's presentation to the assembled group at Jordan College at the beginning of *The Golden Compass* was not a public lecture. Indeed, the knowledge that Lord Asriel was acquiring was considered sufficiently dangerous that the Master of Jordan College tried to poison him.

What is the danger in segregating knowledge in a select group of people? If one group controls knowledge, then they are also in a position to mandate the solution of ethical dilemmas. Consider, for example, the desire on the part of the Church in Lyra's world to understand what happens when a person is severed from his or her dæmon. Because the Church was the only institution that knew about this branch of science, they were able to decide for themselves that this research could be carried out without regard to the dangers it posed for the people who were the subjects of the study. They could decide that the benefit of acquiring knowledge was worth the destruction of a few lives.

The segregation of knowledge in an elite class of people in Lyra's Oxford had grave consequences. However, the broader point here is that Lyra's Oxford is not a dissimilar from our own world as we might like. Knowledge is segregated in our own society too. Our modern world provides much free access to information, but information is like a brain without a body. It does not become knowledge until it is embedded into a system in which it is used. Just as we cannot understand the brain without knowing how it allows us to perceive and act on the world, we cannot truly understand information and turn it into knowledge until we recognize how it was gathered and how it can be used to solve problems.

The willingness of Western science to isolate single variables, to examine people and objects as independent of their environment, has been critical to our development of science. But this becomes a problem when scientific knowledge is released back into society in the form of technology. The subtle knife stands as a warning of the unintentional negative consequences of technology. The knife can be used to cut windows between universes. Repeated use of the knife allowed Specters to travel between worlds, feeding on the souls of adults.

What makes the knife particularly interesting is that it is not inherently evil. Unlike Sauron's ring of power in Tolkein's *The Lord of the Rings*, the knife does not inevitably corrupt its bearer. Indeed, Will and Lyra accomplish a great deal of good using the knife (and other technologies of Lyra's world like the alethiometer). Furthermore, the purpose of the subtle knife is not inherently evil. The ability to travel from one parallel universe to another seems ethically neutral.

It is the use of this technology indiscriminately without regard to the more global universe that is the problem. When holes are left between worlds, Specters escape and travel among worlds, feeding on the souls of adults. These potential side effects were not considered when the knife was developed and used, and were only recognized later when the danger became apparent.

Unintentional side effects of technology are quite common in our world. Some of these consequences are obvious. Creating energy to power our cars, buildings and factories has led to the depletion of natural resources, pollution of our environment and to potentially lethal global warming. Some are less obvious. Creating efficient transportation systems and a global economy has fractured our social structures and disrupted our sense of community. Family members are now able to live far from each other, leading people to feel isolated from their relatives. In both of these examples, however, the negative consequences come from imposing technology on a society rather than allowing it to grow organically.

Pullman recognizes the importance of allowing technology to flower within a society by allowing the technology to evolve in tandem with it. For example, in *The Amber Spyglass* the Mulefa co-evolved with the seedpods that allowed them to travel great distances at high speeds. The seedpods are a kind of technology, but they are benign. The Mulefa live in a kind of ideal world in which animals live in general harmony with their environment. Indeed, Pullman marks this difference in the worlds with the entire palette of the Mulefa's world. It is painted as sunny and bright. That is not to say that there are no predators in this world (the swan-like creatures prey on the Mulefa) but the use of technology in this world allows the creatures to maintain a balance in the world.

The witches in *The Amber Spyglass* also live in tandem with their environment. When Serafina Pekkala heals Will's wound, she does so by communing with the trees. Pullman paints the witches as developing a (magical) technology that is continuous with their environment rather than imposed on it. Even Iorek Byrnison and his race of bears live in greater harmony with their environment than do the men around them. Iorek can be powerful and violent, but he makes use of the materials around him to fashion his armor, and—like the witches and the Mulefa—he does not reshape the environment in unnatural ways.

So, technology can be a force for good, but it must be grown within the structure of a culture rather than imposed on it. The unintended side effects of technology require a consideration of the relationship between the technology and the broader culture.

This analysis suggests that the forces that create technology and those that should govern its introduction are not the same. Science breeds technology, but science advances by extracting objects from their environment in order to determine the causal structure of the universe. The introduction of technology into the world, however, is a sociological problem. It requires understanding the relationship of that technology to the people and societies that will use it.

That means that, in our own world, we need to be more careful about how we test the influence of technology on our world. Scientific method would say that we should try to isolate the influence of a technology on society. For example, we can study the influence of television on education by exploring how much television children watch and examining its relationship to grades and performance on standardized tests. However, really understanding how a technological advance influences society requires attending to the relationships between the technology and other elements of our social structure. Uncovering the influences of television on education requires understanding the role that television plays within the modern family. These kinds of analyses cannot be done by isolating television as an independent factor that affects education, but rather by using relational methods to place the technology its proper context. These methods can be used prospectively as well, to examine how the introduction of a technology may influence the people who will use it.

So, my son was right. Pullman did bury a simple model of consciousness into his dæmons. Pantalaimon is an embodiment of Lyra's homunculus who views her Cartesian Theater. Of course, humans have no actual homunculus. Instead, in a way that is still a mystery to us, the brain provides each of us with a conscious experience of the world around us. The most recent work on embodied cognition may provide important insights into how the mind is actually organized.

Though Pullman may have played with a simple model of consciousness, his views on the relationship between knowledge, science, technology and society are much deeper. He provides both the cautionary examples of the unintended dangers of technology as well as the examples of technology's organic development within a culture. Implementing those ideas in our own society will require focusing on relationships between technology and society that go beyond the nature of the science that spurs technological development.

Sources

The following works were used to develop the ideas in this essay.

Clark, A. (1996). *Being There: Putting Brain, Body, and World Together Again.* Cambridge, MA: The MIT Press.

Dennett, D. C. (1991). *Consciousness Explained.* Boston, MA: Little, Brown, and Company.

Dennett, D. C., & Kinsbourne, M. (1992). Time and the observer: The where and when of consciousness in the brain. *Behavioral and Brain Sciences, 15,* 183–247.

Nisbett, R. E., Peng, K., Choi, I., & Norenzayan, A. (2001). Culture and systems of thought: Holistic and analytic cognition. *Psychological Review, 108,* 291–301.

Arthur B. Markman is a professor of psychology and marketing at the University of Texas, Austin. He received his Ph.D. in 1992 from the University of Illinois and worked at Northwestern University and Columbia University before moving to Texas. He has written over eighty scholarly works. He is a past executive officer of the Cognitive Science Society. He is also a member of the scientific advisory board for The Dr. Phil Show.

KIM DOLGIN

Coming of Age in Svalbard, and Beyond

A wonderful aspect of literature is that everyone brings something of his or her own into the reading of the text. As I am a developmental psychologist, what struck me most strongly about Philip Pullman's His Dark Materials trilogy is that it is a delightful "coming of age" story. This is especially true of Lyra, who begins as a willful, self-centered child, flies through the development normally associated with adolescence and ends as a caring, responsible young adult. (If the time frame within which this occurs is considerably accelerated and unnaturally precocious, well, these are fantasy novels.) Will, conversely, is a child-adult from his introduction in the second novel with one significant exception: he does not mature—he does not need to mature—to the same degree as does Lyra.

At the beginning of the book Lyra is most certainly childlike. Everyone around her, even her dæmon, agrees. "Spying is for silly children..." Pantalaimon chides her early on. "... and I think it would be the silliest thing in a lifetime of silly things to interfere." "Why should a distant theological riddle interest a healthy, thoughtless child?" muses a Scholar. Lyra is consumed with her wars against rival groups of children, spitting plum pits on the heads of passing Scholars and disrupting instruction by hooting, owl-like, outside of classrooms. Her interests do not go beyond relieving her own boredom, dodging her lessons and establishing her place in the juvenile pecking order. Events, however, quickly begin to widen her horizons beyond her own rather petty concerns.

At the age of eleven or twelve, Lyra and Will are just at the threshold of early adolescence. Most people correctly associate these years with the advent of puberty, and that is certainly one of the most important changes that occurs at this time. One's body begins to sexually mature: hair sprouts, (female) breasts bud and (male) musculature takes on definition. Surges in the hormones DHEA and testosterone, respectively, give rise to both romantic and sexual desires. Much of *The Amber Spyglass* is concerned with this aspect of Lyra and Will's development, but adolescence is a time of myriad other behavioral evolutions as well, many of which are portrayed in the first two novels in addition to the third.

Several of the transformations that occur during adolescence are outgrowths of the formidable cognitive development that takes place during the teenage years. Pre-adolescent children use a style of thinking that the great Swiss psychologist, Jean Piaget, termed "concrete operations." Although much advanced over the cognitive patterns exhibited by younger children, pre-adolescents nonetheless are hampered by numerous cognitive limitations. For example, they can only conceptualize the reality they have witnessed as opposed to the possibilities that might be. They fall back upon a relatively small repertoire of behaviors that have served them well in the past. They are boxed in by their inability to logically manipulate information counter to their own experiences and they are not very systematic when rummaging through information to find what they need.

This changes during adolescence, at which time individuals enter the stage of reasoning Piaget called "formal operations." Adolescents, but not children, can think about the abstract (good, evil, God, the spirit behind rules) as well as the concrete (the letter of the law, immediate consequences). They ask themselves "what if..." questions and ponder ways to improve the world by changing the status quo. Their ability to generate novel, untried solutions to problems blossoms: they can now think out of the box. Teenagers are not content to take things at face value, and instead look under the surface. While children passively accept what authority figures tell them, adolescents do not.

By the end of the series, Lyra's and Will's thinking exemplifies formal operational reasoning in a number of ways. Although in the beginning they operate at the concrete level, siding for or against specific individuals ("good" is "my dad," "bad" is "the Gobblers"), by the third novel they worry about whether what they are doing is *right*. They readily accept the existence of forces that are invisible and intangible (Dust, Specters). They devise intricate, multi-step plans to accomplish their ends, such as Lyra's arranging the downfall of Iofur Raknison or Will's scheme to rescue the sleeping Lyra.

Still, formal operations is not the highest level of reasoning, and Lyra and Will are constrained by its limitations. They tend to see conflicts in terms of absolutes: persons are Good or Evil, positions are Right or Wrong. They see the world in dualities. Their viewpoints do not allow for subtlety, gray areas or middle grounds, only extremities and bipolarities. While the reader and several of the older characters may appreciate some degree of murkiness—for example, Mrs. Coulter is largely evil but does fight for her daughter in the end, and the armored bear Iorek Byrnison is the first to realize that the subtle knife has purposes of its own, causing harm when none is intended—the protagonists do not. Indeed, in their minds even the malevolent Harpies miraculously transform to become agents of pure virtue after Will cuts an exit out of the land of the dead: they cannot be seen as both foul and fair at the same time. Will and Lyra have not yet attained *dialectical reasoning*, the ability to incorporate conflicting information, nor should they by their age.

The cognitive advances that come with formal operations cause predictable personality changes in adolescents. For example, many young teenagers develop what David Elkind termed "the personal fable." That is, they believe that no one else can truly understand them. They believe that they are deeper, more intensely feeling and more perceptive than everyone else around them. While Lyra loves and is grateful for Pan, it is in good part because she believes that he alone can fully understand and appreciate her. Since Pan is an aspect of Lyra herself, her spirit, that belief is quintessentially egocentric. In addition, the new ability to see unrealized alternatives leads many adolescents to become idealistic, desirous of changing the world for the better and convinced that they can be instrumental in bringing such alterations about. Lyra and Will, of course, are prepared to bring about events that will transform the fundamental nature of death itself, and they have no qualms about taking part in a war that will reshape the celestial order of their universe. Also, as an outgrowth of this idealism, many adolescents become what Elkind termed *messianic*; that is, they become hero worshipers of those they think can effect positive change. They find individuals to follow, believing them to be omniscient and worthy of devotion. At various times, Lyra expresses adoration for Mrs. Coulter to Iorek and to Will, seeing no fault in her at the time.

Another important adolescent maturational change that can occur only after the advent of formal operations is the formation of an *identity*. Erik Erikson, arguably the most important developmental psychologist to date, stated that this is *the* central life task of adolescence. To Erikson, who coined the term, having an identity means knowing who you are and what you want out of life. It involves feeling the continuity between the child you once were and the adult you wish to be. It means that you are your own person, capable of making your own decisions, and that you have developed a coherent set of values to guide your behavioral choices. Developing an identity involves making hundred of choices—in Erikson's terms, resolving hundreds of crises—that together constitute your life plan. The best way to make these choices is to "try on different hats," to behave in many different ways until you the find the way that best suits you. By seeing how each option feels and by observing others' reactions to you, you settle on the patterns that suit you. Again, this process is possible only after a person is capable of engaging in the hypothetical and abstract thought that comes in with formal operations, and hence begins in adolescence.

In His Dark Materials, one's dæmon represents a number of important constructs, including the identity. "They have always settled, and they always will. That's part of growing up. There'll come a time when you'll be tired of his changing about, and you'll want a settled kind of form for him." This fact is initially inconceivable to Lyra, who relishes Pantalaimon's shape-shifting (and, hence, her own fluidity). However, after she has found herself and become a young woman, she is delighted by the form that Pantalaimon assumes, and says "You remember when we were younger and I didn't want you to stop changing at all... Well, I wouldn't mind so much now. Not if you stay like this." If one has formed a healthy, positive identity, one is content to be himself or herself and feels no longer feels a need to experiment or change.

Forging an independent identity rests not only upon sufficient cognitive sophistication, but also on the ability to break away from one's parents. An adolescent must learn to tolerate parental disapproval if he or she is going to become a unique individual, rather than a clone. The mental development associated with formal operations allows the normal process of distancing process to begin: while children are rather incapable of seeing their parents as anything less than perfect, adolescents have no trouble viewing maternal and paternal feet of clay. Hypothetical reasoning, with its "what if...?" questioning, allows adolescents to challenge their parents' behaviors within their own minds. The newfound ability to generate creative alternatives allows them to answer their own questions with what appear to be superior rejoinders. Not everything Mom and Dad say is best! And, since formal thought is characterized by all-or-none reasoning, if Mom and Dad aren't always right then they must be only rarely right. At times Lyra actively fights against the wishes of both her mother and her father; Will has long ago recognized his mother's flaws.

Good parents foster the kind of independence needed for identity formation; they do not require their children to follow, lockstep, in their footsteps and they encourage autonomy. Unfortunately, Lyra is not blessed with anything approaching good parents. Her father more or less ignores her and her mother (once she belatedly begins to take an interest) wants her to become "foreclosed." Foreclosed individuals behave the way their parents want them to behave, have the values and live the lives their parents want them to have. Parents who encourage their children to become foreclosed often do so by being kind and loving only when their children do exactly what their parents desire; as soon as a child in any way deviates from the laid-down path, he or she is harshly punished. This is unquestionably the tactic Mrs. Coulter uses with Lyra: she is all sweetness and kisses when her daughter dresses up and behaves meekly, but her golden monkey viciously attacks Pan when Lyra offers even meager rebellion by refusing to leave her purse in her bedroom.

A final, dramatic aspect of Lyra's maturation that is tied to cognitive development is in her level of moral reasoning. (Will, who has been caring for his mother since the age of seven, begins the book at an already advanced moral stage.) At the start of the story, she is self-centered and egocentric. She does whatever she finds to be fun, and is only obedient so that she can avoid being punished. She is not concerned about how her actions affect others. This corresponds to a level of moral behavior Lawrence Kohlberg called *preconventional moral reasoning*: it is the most primitive form of morality and is characteristic of children's, as well as some adults', behavior. Lyra appears to have skipped the kind of moral reasoning that typically follows, *conventional morality*. If Lyra had ever been a typical conventional moral reasoner, she would have at first cared deeply about what others thought of her; she would have desired other people's approval of her actions. (Only Lyra's behaviors during her brief infatuation with Mrs. Coulter would qualify as *conventional*.) Somewhat later, she would have gone through a period in which she was very concerned with following rules and doing as she was told by authority figures. Instead, our headstrong protagonist remained completely indifferent to others' expectations and charted her own course. In doing so, Lyra bypassed conventional morality and leapt right into *postconventional moral reasoning.* In this final, highest level, she does what she believes is right—even if she has to buck friends and authority figures to do so. She stands up for the greater good and tries to act so that most others in society will benefit from her actions. It is hard to imagine any character being more unmistakably postconventional. Lyra disobeys her parents and her church, which doubles as the governing body of her land, to do what she believes is right; she and Will sacrifice their own happiness for the ghosts of friends and strangers alike, because it helps so many others.

Two other notable personality differences, perhaps less directly tied to cognitive maturation *per se*, exist between children and adults. One is the willingness to assume responsibility for one's actions. Lyra, for example, voluntarily bears the pain of separation from Pantalaimon when she journeys to the land of death because she perceives herself as being responsible for Roger's death, although it is very difficult for her to do so. The second difference lies in the ways in which children and adults perceive the world. Children experience the world in a pure, unitary manner whereas adults' perceptions are muted and complex. (Hence the word "adulterated.") These changes are a result of both cognitive maturation as well as the accumulated weight of memory and experience. As a child, Lyra could eat a red berry and merely revel in its sweetness; the older Lyra, eating the same berry, is delighted by the taste but at the same time saddened by the memory of the last picnic she shared with Will and nostalgic for her time with the Mulefa. Time ages us, but events do so equally. Childhood is sweet or sour; adulthood is bittersweet.

Much of the third novel, *The Amber Spyglass*, deals with Lyra's and Will's awakening sexuality. Threads of this theme, that adults differ from children in that they lack innocence, can of course be seen throughout the entire trilogy. Still, the primary tragic element in Lyra and Will's story, and its culmination, is that they are forced to abandon their new-found romantic love almost as soon as they have discovered it.

As was mentioned before, early adolescence is a time of emerging sexual and romantic longings. A part of this process involves becoming more keenly aware that one is male rather than female, or female rather than male. Gender identification intensifies greatly during the early adolescent years, and children at this age become increasingly interested in taking on the trappings of adult men and women. Indeed, one of the main reasons that Lyra is initially taken with Mrs. Coulter is that she is so essentially female. Lyra's world has been comprised almost entirely of sexless children and old, uninteresting men. (The only women she has previously had any contact with are servants, who are beneath her aristocratic notice, and the occasional visiting female Scholar, who is shapeless and dull.) Mrs. Coulter is beautiful and elegant, and once Lyra is given into her care she begins experimenting with acting like the woman she admires: "There were other kinds of lessons . . . that . . . didn't feel like lessons at all. How to wash one's own hair; how to judge which colors suited one . . . how to put on lipstick, powder, scent." Lyra begins to be more conscious of and self-conscious about her own femininity. For example, at one point in the third novel she thinks to herself that "she happily used to swim naked in the River Cherwell with all the other Oxford children, but it would be quite different with Will" and she blushes at the thought of it.

In a very different way Mrs. Coulter's blatant attractiveness is also instrumental in making Will aware of his own burgeoning maleness. Upon first meeting her, even though he knew she was evil, Will found that "He had been captivated by Mrs. Coulter. All his thoughts referred to her: when he thought of Lyra, it was to wonder how like her mother she'd be when she grew up; if he thought of the Church, it was to wonder how many of the priests and cardinals were under her spell; if he thought of his own dead father, it was to wonder whether he would have detested her or admired her. . . ." It is not at all clear whether Will's platonic feelings for Lyra would have developed into romantic love or would have done so as quickly had he, too, not been touched by the sensuous Mrs. Coulter. When we first meet him, it is quite clear that he is still his mother's little boy; when he reminisces about his relationship with her, he thinks "she was so full of love and sweetness then that he could think of no better companion, and wanted nothing more than to live alone with her forever." He was not yet feeling pulled toward adult, intimate relationships.

In Pullman's world, dæmons are inextricably connected to sexuality as well as to identity. Indeed, since humans are sexual beings, any mature identity acknowledges and embraces one's erotic feelings. Dæmons are viewed as being the direct cause of sexual desires. As Mrs. Coulter instructs Lyra, " . . . at the age we call puberty, the age you're coming to very soon, darling, dæmons bring all sorts of troublesome thoughts and feelings." And, as is often the case in our own world, sexuality is linked with sinfulness. Reading from the Bible, Lord Azriel informs Lyra, "That is how sin came into the world . . . sin and shame and death. It came the moment their dæmons become fixed." And, that is why, during Ruta Skadi's travels, she could find cultures in which children's sexual organs are cut so that they won't experience sexual desire.

Pullman's take on sexuality is in keeping with the "common man" position on the course of sexual development. He and his characters, like most persons, assume that children are completely asexual and that erotic urges do not emerge until puberty. While the truth is perhaps not quite so simple, as even very young children show active interest in viewing other people's bodies and rub their own genitals, children do not crave sexual encounters with other individuals. This view is, though, decidedly counter to one of the most influential perspectives on sexuality, Sigmund Freud's. Sigmund Freud believed that the human psyche consists of three parts: the id, present from birth and the seat of sexual desires; the ego, or rational part of the self, present from later in infancy; and the superego, composed of the conscience (the list of "thou shalt nots" in our minds) and the ego ideal (the list of "thou shalts"), formed by about six years of age. In Freud's view, even infants are sexual—although they express their sexual interest in ways different from adults—and preschoolers are even more so.

In the universe of His Dark Materials, in contrast, characters have chiding, restraining consciences from birth (their dæmons). These dæmons also incorporate aspects of the ego, in that they are portrayed as often more thoughtful than their humans. They morph and become at least partially like ids at puberty. Still, a notable similarity in Pullman's and Freud's zeitgeists exists. According to Freud, the id is fueled and energized by a powerful force called the libido, which galvanizes all human action. Indeed, in Freud's opinion sexual energy is at the heart of all art, entrepreneurship, competition and conquest. Pullman echoes this characterization by imbuing characters with a libido sufficiently potent to attract Dust, the particles of which angels are composed and that which makes us truly sentient. He also describes a reality in which intercision, the severing of dæmon, or id, from person, releases enough energy to blast a hole in the fabric of the universe.

So in myriad ways, Lyra matures during the course of His Dark Materials. In general, Pullman does a fine job of accurately representing the kinds of changes that occur after a person moves out of childhood. The pace and age at which Lyra develops are wildly impossible. At twelve or thirteen, Lyra should just be beginning to progress out of childhood; in most ways she acts like an adult, not even an older adolescent, throughout much of the story. Formal operations is usually not mastered until mid- or late-adolescence, and belief in the personal fable lingers for at least a few years. Identity formation continues well into one's twenties, while postconventional moral reasoning virtually never occurs until the very late teens or early twenties at the earliest. The ability to assume responsibility for one's actions is most certainly not a hallmark of early adolescence; indeed, some individuals never acquire this trait, even as adults. Will and Lyra are precocious sexually and romantically as well: most thirteen-year-olds restrict their cross-sex interactions with those to whom they are attracted to giggling (girls) or showing off (boys). Even if they had the opportunity to act on romantic desires, typical twelve-year-olds would generally be too shy and self-conscious to do much more than hold hands. "True love" to the average early adolescent usually lasts about two weeks, not a lifetime. Still, modern physics tells us that time runs differently in parallel universes, and so too might maturation.

Kim Gale Dolgin is a professor of psychology at Ohio Wesleyan University. She received her B.A., two M.A.s and Ph.D. from the University of Pennsylvania. She teaches courses in adolescent and child development as well as human sexuality. Her research interests include parent-adolescent "friendship" in late adolescence, sibling relationships, children's understanding of emotional pain and the development of higher order, complex reasoning skills. She is coauthor, together with Philip Rice, of the textbook The Adolescent: Development, Relationships, and Culture, *now in its eleventh edition. Dr. Dolgin has received both of her university's outstanding teaching awards. She is an avid, long-standing reader of both fantasy and science fiction and would have named her children after Tolkien characters had her husband permitted.*

KAREN TRAVISS

I Gotta Get Me One of Those:
Why Dæmons Might Make the World a Better Place

Location: a pub, somewhere in the city.
"Is that your dæmon?"
"Yeah. He's a registered pit-bull, but he's great with the kids."
"What's his name, then?"
"Tyson."
"Don't you find him a bit ... embarrassing?"
"No. Why?"
"Well, not many hairdressers have pit-bulls for dæmons. ..."

Every writer needs a Bloody Good Idea.

You can tell the difference between a Bloody Good Idea (BGI) and a McGuffin because the BGI is often the one facet that you still recall and savor years after you've forgotten the rest of the story. That doesn't necessarily mean that the story isn't as big as the idea, of course, or that the story is lacking, or that the BGI isn't integral to the plot. It might just be that the idea is just so Bloody Good that it can stand on its own, apart from the book, and—more importantly—that it grips the imagination of the reader.

Pullman's dæmons fall into that category.

Ask most non-academic readers what aspect of the His Dark Materials trilogy springs to mind, and they'll say *dæmons*. We've all thought it: what would our own dæmon be like? In the office where I used to work, a colleague confessed to spending her daily train journey ascribing different dæmons to fellow passengers. If dæmons had been available by

81

mail order, she'd have bought one for herself there and then. Dæmons are more than a good fiction device: they answer a need in us, though not always a positive one.

Whether we see them as the external manifestation of our souls, as in the book, is another matter. Part of their appeal is probably more as a fashion accessory, a pet, an uncritical friend or even an alter ego. But we toy with the idea of having one without thinking too hard about what it might mean if one manifested itself on our shoulder here and now in the real world.

In Pullman's universe the characters accept their dæmons; in ours I suspect we'd have a much harder time coming to terms with their implications and visibility. We would be superimposing dæmons on a society steeped in imagery and visual grammar that all too often shows us that what you see isn't actually what you get. But if we did try dæmons for size, I suspect we'd all do some growing up once the novelty wore off.

Remember, you can't choose your dæmon. And when you grow up, you can't change it—and it's with you 24/7.

Society would have to adapt.

> *"So, Mr. Silver. What attracts you to this job?"*
> *"Arrr, it's not me so much me, matey, it's me dæmon's idea."*
> *"Yes, he's a very fine macaw, Mr. Silver."*
> *"He's always bin wantin' to work with computer programmin' see,*
> *   on account of 'is bein' able to count in the octal system."*
> *"I don't quite follow you, Mr. Silver."*
> *"Cap'n Flint's very keen on pieces of eight."*

Dæmons now abound, and become an immediate aid to human resources professionals.

It's a vast improvement on the pre-dæmon days, which you recall with a shudder. In a pile of coffee-spattered, dreary applications that didn't even meet the personal spec, you found one, perhaps two, that looked like the answer to your prayers. You called the candidates for interview. They dressed for success, they talked a good game and they had terrific ideas for taking your business forward.

Then you offered one of them the job, and within a few days of their taking up the post you found you were saddled with the Employee from Hell.

They didn't get on with the rest of the team, their resume proved to be a little upholstered, and their last employer was so keen to get rid of them that they gave them a reference that would win the Whitbread prize for fiction. And they had nasty habits.

It took you a year to unload them onto another unsuspecting company, a year that sapped your will to live.

Recruitment and selection with dæmons is a huge step forward.

The apparently ideal candidate's dæmon is a hyena. He's tried to dress it up as a Labrador to exude reliable friendliness, but it laughs at all the wrong points in the interview. It savages another candidate's baby antelope dæmon while they're taking their personality profile tests. And at the embarrassing buffet lunch when your team has to meet their prospective colleagues, it gets into a fight with the receptionist's lion dæmon.

It's never going to work out, but you know before you sign on the line. See how much time you've saved?

> "I dumped him, of course."
> "Married, then?"
> "Yeah. Thought I wouldn't find out. But his dæmon was this little weasel that kept looking at its watch."
> "You can always tell, can't you?"
> "Yeah. Men...."

With a dæmon, you have no choice but to be honest in your relationships.

In many ways, the dæmon can complicate romantic matters—does his dæmon get on with yours as well as you do with him?—but on balance, dæmons help more than they hinder. There's no more need to find out if your intended was born in the Year of the Monkey or under Capricorn. You can see instantly if you're about to start dating a skunk.

If you're too shy to make the first move, your dæmon can help you strike up a conversation in the park or by the water cooler better than any mutt. And it won't embarrass you by embracing your fancy's leg in the awful manner of amorous small dogs. (Unless, of course, your dæmon is a Jack Russell.)

The downside of dæmons is always what they reveal about you, but that's a boon for the nervous or suspicious romantic wondering if Mister or Miss Right is actually an axe murderer. They can be a liability if you're trying to enhance your own image, though. Your dæmon, aging as you do, needs the same sprucing up each time you opt for Botox or the scalpel.

But it's no bad thing if your dæmon is a glamorous creature like a peacock or a cheetah. Just remember, though, that some of us will manifest as a tortoise or a leech.

And there are no dæmon transplants.

We won't go into the in-laws' dæmonology. It's never going to be good. On the other hand, the flapping wings of the vulture dæmon that heralds your mother-in-law's arrival give you valuable seconds to whip out that hideous vase she bought you and make sure it's prominently displayed before you open the door.

And if you're getting over a broken heart, your dæmon is someone who'll listen patiently to your most intimate fear and pain and keep you company while you watch a weepy movie. Your dæmon is your uncritical, faithful, supportive friend who requires no apology or explanation.

You can see why dæmons are proving so popular.

Is your dæmon looking as run down and listless as you are? Lost your sparkle? Then you both need to start the day with a delicious blend of live acidophilus and yogurt....

Dæmons prove to be good for the economy too.

Sooner or later, we become dissatisfied with aspects of our dæmon, and dissatisfaction means expenditure. We might not want to actually change the dæmon, but we'd like to give it a fresh new look. We're creatures of trend. Like the latest gadget, our dæmon might simply make us feel that we're somehow lacking and that a change of appearance or style—any change—would boost our morale.

So dæmons suddenly spawn a whole line of merchandising, from coats that complement your dæmon ermine or fox to studded collars and matching human-dæmon accessories. It's all rather redolent of the consumer industry that accompanies pampered pets, full of excess and irony, and the marketing and advertising people—who *all* have tapeworms for dæmons, albeit ones in designer colors—know how to play to our anxieties.

The wannabe tough guy is tempted into buying a leather harness for his kitten dæmon because he's finding it a little hard to be taken seriously in the pub. The woman who longs to be an impossible size 0 really has to do something about her homely cart-horse dæmon, although it's hard to make it look anything less than solid and pragmatic. And there's not a lot you can do with a tarantula dæmon, apart from buying a tasteful cover for it, although it guarantees you plenty of space to yourself on public transport.

You can see that in the twenty-first-century Western world, we don't find this dæmon thing quite as much fun as we first imagined. It's not easy to accept that an unchanging summary of your entire personality, a living icon, accompanies you visibly wherever you go.

A dæmon says more about you than your choice of credit card ever can.

"It's your mother's fault."
"What's my mother got to do with it?"
"If she hadn't mollycoddled the kid, he'd have a better dæmon."
"So he's got a rabbit. What's wrong with that?"
"When he was little he had a dragon and a tiger. How's he going to look in the boardroom with a damn rabbit?"

Unlike Pullman's characters, we often don't live in comfortable acceptance of our dæmons. Once the novelty of a walking, talking projection of our innermost selves wears off, we slip into our old habits and establish prejudices and pecking orders based on external appearance and assumption.

The dæmon, of course, is a shorthand guide to what's actually within: we forget they're a manifestation of our soul. But there are many creatures whose appearance and image don't match their qualities. There are still few of us in the West—and even fewer in the Middle East—who want an intelligent, friendly and courageous *pig* as a dæmon.

We fail, as always, to look beneath the surface and revert to our pattern-recognizing instinct to categorize and exclude. Why do our dæmons take the forms they do? Are they expressing *real* aspects of the totemic animal, or the ones we ascribe to it without knowing the facts about its behavior in the wild? Is the dæmon the projection of our prejudices, or determined by an independent, objective assessment of the nature of the animal?

At this point, I consider my options. I'm not sure I'd want a lion dæmon, not if I was mixing with zoologists. The mane is impressive, I grant you that. But lions, far from being the symbol of manly courage and honor foisted on us by heraldry, are bone-idle, let their females do all the serious work and slaughter cubs who've been fathered by another male. And I'd steer clear of dolphins if I could, too: rape, gang violence, bullying and child murder lie beneath their perma-smiling, intelligent exterior.

You're judged by your dæmon. And different people judge it in unexpected ways.

"I'm sorry, I don't want you bringing her home."
"Why? I love her."
"She's got a dog dæmon."
"It's just an icon. Dogs are seen as loyal and affectionate in her culture."
"And in ours, dogs are unclean. I insist you marry a doe."

It's all getting a little uncomfortable now that we've had dæmons in this universe for a while. Since people have realized how very permanent a dæmon is, and the impact it can have on your career and standing in society, a new type of therapist springs up.

They specialize in helping children manifest the best dæmon at puberty, the dæmon that makes them winners, makes them *attractive*. Kids who felt comforted by their rabbit or their stick insect or their snail are under pressure to make Mummy and Daddy proud of them by trying very hard to project a gazelle or a bull. The kid with an increasing affection for a much-loved mouse dæmon is having a very difficult time with his career-military father, who'd really like him to shape up into a panther and join the infantry.

Inevitably, the pressure from cruel well-meaning parents creates personalities that manifest unhappy dæmons as adults. Is it really surprising that the tubby little girl being "helped" to project an elegant swan finds herself battling with a bear who gorges all summer and then starves herself for months?

Fortunately, child-dæmon experts then appear in the media warning parents of the dangers of trying to force kids into dæmon forms that they can't possibly attain.

Sensible parents, though, are happy with whatever form their child's dæmon takes, and oddly enough, they tend to manifest as contented calves. As a result, research studies are funded to explain the obvious.

The Old Bailey, London.
"Challenge."
"Counsel, this is your tenth challenge to a juror this morning."
"They have a cat dæmon, M'Lord. I believe it would prejudice my client's trial."

The dæmon at law gives us more pressing issues. Lawyers—and you can spot them easily in the street by their leech or jackal dæmon—have quickly learned that certain manifestations guarantee a conviction. Would any jury believe the man with the gorilla dæmon didn't start the brawl, but was simply defending himself? Fortunately the legal aid system means that those with violent-looking dæmons can still get representation because the lawyer gets paid regardless of the verdict. Those who don't qualify for aid had better hope they manifest as a white dove.

Assumptions continue to have an impact on people's lives even after they've served their sentence and returned to society. The woman with a magpie on her shoulder finds it hard to get *any* job after she's served two years for embezzlement. She says she's learned her lesson and has put her criminal past behind her, but her dæmon conveys a silent, subliminal message to all who see her; he can never change.

Inevitably, the police and the intelligence community begin to take a great interest in attempts to circumvent identification by dæmon. The witness protection program watches nervously.

"So you don't feel good about yourself."
"No, Doctor. I feel inadequate."
"It's not so bad having a shrew as a dæmon."
"It makes me look small and stupid."
"Think of it another way. Shrews live life in the fast lane; they're always ready for a fight and they really enjoy their food."
"I'd never looked at it that way before, Doctor. Thank you."

Confronting yourself has now become far easier thanks to dæmons.

After years of treating them as buddies and fashion statements, and then understanding them as an all too public revelation about our inner selves, we've started to come to terms with them, and with the dæmons of others.

We can't change them. We can look back and wonder what might have been if our childhood had been different and the malleable part of our character could have been shaped to something attractive, or heroic, or quirky: we can long for better-looking and sexier dæmons. But our dæmons are what we are, and rather than blame the past and decide we're now bound by it, we can do what tribal peoples have done for centuries, and look for the qualities in every animal manifestation to influence how we live out each day.

Dæmons are also a great leveler. Good nutrition, health and cosmetic treatments may buy you looks, but no amount of money can purchase a different dæmon. As soon as we give up the pursuit of ways to alter our dæmons, we learn to accept them and we become less judgmental about others. We recognize common dæmon forms that we share with those who don't look like us, speak like us, or believe what we believe and focus on similarities rather than difference.

I think I could enjoy living in a world with dæmons. And mine's a brown rat, by the way. I knew you'd have to ask.

Karen Traviss is a British author whose debut sf novels City of Pearl *and* Crossing The Line *(Eos) received critical acclaim when they were published in the USA in 2004. A former defense correspondent and TV and newspaper journalist, she now lives in Wiltshire.*

JEAN RABE

Letter to the Editor: In Praise of Mrs. Coulter

To *The London Times*
ATTENTION: Editorial Section

Dear Sirs:

As an avid reader of your once-fine newspaper, I find myself increasingly displeased with your articles concerning Mrs. Coulter's behavior and her research into the matter of Dust. You have sullied her fine name by unduly criticizing her character and activities! Your coverage is biased and erroneous, quoting individuals who claim that she is a menace to society, children in particular. On the contrary, she is a boon to both, as I shall explain:

Beautiful, intelligent, gracious and graceful—Mrs. Coulter is all of those things and much more. A caring mother, a competent ally, a sophisticated social butterfly, she has boundless fine qualities that distinguished her from her Oxford peers. Her home is grand and immaculate, her parties lavish and her guest list impressive—I can attest to these things, as I have been a guest in her home on more than one occasion. She wears the finest clothes, exhibits impeccable manners and she has an extraordinary dæmon in the little monkey with the gold, silky coat.

Some—the quick to judge and the slow to evaluate (including your reporters)—would paint her a villain for the acts she commits involving children. These observers are unable to look at the broader view. The discriminating souls able to place society before the individual would certainly see that Mrs. Coulter is a boon to humanity and that suitable praise should be heaped upon this esteemed icon.

Significantly Lowering the Crime and Disease Rate

Mrs. Coulter does not abscond with children from the high ranks of society, or even from upper middle-income homes. Rather, she endeavors to take children from the poorest of parents, crude ragamuffins who playfully skitter through alleys like grubby rats and whose presence despoils the city's otherwise picturesque image. These children are largely unwashed and uneducated, and would no doubt turn to thievery to feed themselves and their siblings—if they haven't already begun such a heinous practice. There is little chance they will grow to become respectable members of society and contribute something for the betterment of their fellow men. Instead, children like these will indubitably grow into homeless adults, wrapped in poverty and living off scraps of food and coins begged from mercilessly hounded passersby.

Untaught, they will never gain jobs that pay well and will never contribute to society. They will marry in their own lowly class, producing more ragamuffins to leech off the respectable folk. Mrs. Coulter's kidnappings help to lessen this vicious, pitiable circle and clean up the streets.

The more ruthless among any such children will turn to serious offenses such as murder to stay fed and clothed. They might be caught breaking into the homes of upstanding people, stealing goods and money, damaging property in the process and making the neighborhoods feel forever unsafe. The greater number of poor, desperate children left to grow to adulthood and to add to this crime wave, the more threatened all the neighborhoods will become.

By getting horrid children such as these off the streets, Mrs. Coulter is lessening the unlawful element in Oxford and elsewhere, making the communities secure and more pleasing places to live. And she is doing this—single-handedly—more productively than any force of police officers or social workers or flock of well-meaning priests. She never charges for her services even though her kidnappings save communities untold amounts of money. And she never seeks recognition for her work. Rather, she humbly keeps to the shadows, striving the proverbial day in and day out to kidnap just enough children to meet her needs (and in the process meet the needs of a vexed society). She is, in effect, a charitable, one-woman crusade to improve the well-being and magnificence of Oxford and the surrounding communities. All the better that she is accomplishing her personal goals in the process.

If only the politicians and law enforcement agencies knew of the repercussions of her activities—they would laud her efforts at community beautification. But that would require your once-impartial newspaper to print her side of the issues. There is still time for your reporters and editors to make amends!

Picture it: cities without armies of dirty urchins underfoot begging from or picking the pockets of honest, hard-working citizens. Filthy children foster the spread of illnesses and lice, so fewer filthy children means a healthier population. And a healthier city will be forced to spend less money on doctors and departments that deal with those poor individuals who cannot pay for the dispensed services. All of this progress will be due to one astute woman who elects to steal a few raggedy children from Oxford's alleys.

Saving All of Society Money

Her activities, which the unthinking will call nefarious or monstrous, are also saving the common folk a considerable amount in taxes. Fewer derelicts and criminals means less money will have to be collected and directed to expanding jails and homeless shelters. Indeed, it is possible some of these institutions could be closed, turned into apartments and shops and theaters. The coins instead could be directed to expanding parks, improving schools and bolstering the arts—enriching all the cultural aspects of Oxford society without raising taxes to do so.

In short, when Mrs. Coulter kidnaps the motley assortment of poor children, she is performing yet one more public service—giving the government an opportunity to redirect its funds to cultural and educational affairs. How sophisticated a country could be, spending its money to enlighten its people rather than to confine and feed the worst of them!

Improving the Lot of Poor Families

Though Mrs. Coulter is bettering all of society through her kidnappings and other dealings, I reiterate that she is most benefiting the poor. She is doing what government agencies and churches cannot—she is making life better for the low-income people.

By stealing only one child from poor parents, Mrs. Coulter is easing the financial burden on that entire family. No longer will coins have to be spent on the now-absent child. Instead, that paltry bit of money can go toward better feeding and clothing for the rest of the brood, giving each remaining child more, and thereby making each happier and healthier. Or the money can be put aside for better living accommodations, eventually moving the family into a less slovenly neighborhood and perhaps getting them out of poverty altogether. Losing one child to Mrs. Coulter in exchange for the chance to climb out of the slums is a small price indeed.

If, by chance, Mrs. Coulter accidentally absconds with the only child such a poor family has, she is improving their finances more than a little. The mother will no longer have to stay home to take care of the child (when said child isn't out roaming the streets and begging). She can find gainful employment and save her wages so she can afford to have another child later when her situation improves. Better to bring a child into a solvent family than into one in dire financial straits. Or perhaps the mother will wisely realize the folly of adding a hungry mouth to a poor household, there being more than enough poor children in the world. With both parents given the opportunity to work, because of Mrs. Coulter's acts, they will have twice the chance to remove themselves from the bottom rung of society.

Initially, of course, parents and remaining siblings—perhaps neighborhoods as a whole—will pine for the absent children. It will be a natural thing to miss abducted relatives and friends. But the mourning will pass, and in its place will arise a stronger, closer family—one more financially sound—and one with parents who will pay closer attention to the remaining offspring.

Parents who lose one child to Mrs. Coulter and "the Gobblers" will likely keep tighter rein on any remaining ones—if they truly care for their brood. As a result, there will be fewer ragamuffins running the streets and bothering the good people of Oxford.

Providing for the Kidnapped Children

Mrs. Coulter steals the children gently, using guile and her golden monkey dæmon. Little force is needed, and so the worst a child suffers is a few scrapes and bruises... likely less than he will have suffered playing in the alleys with his dirty friends.

Children taken by Mrs. Coulter are blessed!

Shortly after their abduction they are placed with others of their kind, in a warm dry room where they are safe from the elements. Further, they are given more and better food than their families have been providing. Fellowship and sustenance...things the little beggars should be grateful for.

A Loving Mother

In addition to helping society as a whole, Mrs. Coulter managed to find time to show great compassion for her daughter Lyra by taking the girl from her orphanage-existence at Jordan College and giving her a true home. Mrs. Coulter sacrificed much of her own personal freedom to take the child in; as I've mentioned above, children require a substantial amount of time and effort if they are to be brought up properly.

Mrs. Coulter saw that Lyra had her own room, a fine comfortable bed and all the delicate and fancy accoutrements a girl could need. Mrs. Coulter bought her new clothes, shoes and accessories and took her through the city, showing Lyra things the child had not seen before, exposing her to the upper crust of Oxford society. She took Lyra to a beautician to have the child's hair and nails done—Lyra had never been pampered so much before. Further, despite Mrs. Coulter's pressing schedule with the "Gobblers" and the business of culling ragamuffins, she managed to find time to school Lyra.

Mrs. Coulter taught Lyra how to wash her hair, how to select colors that suited her and how to apply makeup and cologne. She taught the child manners, which certainly had been lacking up to this point. How more caring and loving could a busy mother be?

When Lyra foolishly fled, Mrs. Coulter worried terribly and could not find peace until they were reunited far to the north—in the place where the kidnapped children had been taken. There, Mrs. Coulter would not allow Lyra to be treated as the other children—those lesser scallywags from Oxford's slums—and therefore she would not think of separating Lyra and her dæmon. (Not that the process of dæmon-separation was beneath Lyra, as perhaps the child could have benefited from it.) But it was likely Mrs. Coulter simply wanted to spare Lyra the pain...the child had experienced enough turmoil already. So Mrs. Coulter protected Lyra as any good mother would.

Later, after Lyra stupidly escaped the northern fortress and made her way to another world, Mrs. Coulter again found her. Lucky for Lyra!

Mrs. Coulter risked everything to keep her daughter safe, going so far as to drug Lyra and hide her in a cave. No threat was too great to face, as far as Mrs. Coulter was concerned. After all, Lyra might be the world's next "Eve" and Mrs. Coulter took it upon herself to keep the child from being snatched by evil forces...though it pained her greatly to in effect hold Lyra prisoner. Few mothers would make such emotional sacrifices for a troublesome little girl. Fewer mothers would leave their fine home and native world for one unappreciative child.

Advancing Science

Your reporters have implied that Mrs. Coulter's laboratory in the far north, where kidnapped children are taken, is the place she perpetrates foul acts. Not so! Nothing vile goes on at that research station; I'm certain of it! At the compound the children are clothed and fed and freely socialized. Their existence is far more pleasant than the life they led on the streets of Oxford and elsewhere. They are clean, never hungry, never wanting for companionship.

Too, the captive children should be honored that Mrs. Coulter selects them for her experiments. It is a chance for them to contribute to the scientific knowledge about Dust, dæmons and how it all connects to people. Some pain might be involved in the process of severing child from dæmon, but sacrifices must be made if there are to be advancements. Any suffering a child feels is nothing in the overall scheme of things. Certainly, a few of the children die after the procedure, but such is to be expected with any important research project. And who is to say they wouldn't have died at a young age anyway to some malady or other? Or starved? There certainly is a good chance they would have succumbed to disease or died to violence had they been left to run the streets of Oxford. The entire severing operation might be no more painful or uncomfortable than a trip to the dentist's office.

So I believe that the children who had their dæmons severed were blessed! They now have the chance to experience life on their own, free of the supernatural entities that were continually changing shape and clinging so closely. They can face the world without a spiritual hanger-on, can make decisions without fear of offending their dæmon or without the need to question that dæmon about this act or that.

Bordering on Sainthood

Mrs. Coulter's acts border on sainthood. She is a true hero on so many levels, and your reporters and editors should be chastised for casting her in an unfavorable light. She sets an example to all of Oxford, and if you accurately reported her travails, the public would embrace her wit and set great store by her brilliance.

Jean Rabe is the author of fifteen fantasy novels and three dozen fantasy, science fiction and military short stories. A former newspaper reporter, she spends her days happily writing about fictional violence. In her spare time, she visits museums filled with old planes, attempts to garden and tugs fiercely on knotted socks with her two dogs. Visit her Web site at www.jeanrabe.com.

KAY KENYON

Reading by Flashlight
What Fantasy Writers Can Learn from Pullman

Hey, what's with this Philip Pullman hijacking fantastic literature and taking a gazillion readers along for the ride? Whether among young readers or adults, Pullman's trilogy is sending people into a buying—and reading—frenzy. Proclaimed by some reviewers as an adult read worthy of our best literature, His Dark Materials is nothing less than a smashing commercial and artistic success.

Literary acclaim, best seller lists...all for a young adult story filled with magic and strange new worlds. It isn't fair! complain my fellow science fiction and fantasy writers. We do all this stuff, and languish in what amounts to a literary ghetto. What is so different about this fantasy story?

Based on first impressions I am tempted to say, not much. We writers of speculative fiction have covered Pullman's fictional ground before, and often as well.

I can hear the protests: Aren't you forgetting Pullman's lucid prose, the originality of his story and its milieu? And how about those startling ideas? Surely these things explain Pullman's legions of fans.

I agree His Dark Materials is a wonderful read. I loved it, and press the books into the hands of the uninitiated, believe me. But that doesn't explain why The Golden Compass vaulted onto the best seller lists while most science fiction and fantasy doesn't. If success was solely based on finely turned prose, how can we explain why Gene Wolfe isn't a household name? Or M. John Harrison? As to the point about Pullman's challenging themes, well, our whole genre prides itself on that sort of thing.

In fact, writers of fantastic literature take some comfort in the notion that our small readership is a reaction to our genre's radical ideas. Most people, after all, don't like their beliefs challenged; they don't like weird ideas, or at least they don't shell out twenty-five dollars for the privilege of reading about them. But Pullman has proved us wrong. By the time we are finishing up the third book in the series we relish the idea that God is an evil old man who's forgotten we exist, that we can still love parents who betray us, that sensuality is good for teenagers, never mind adults.

Yes, Philip Pullman has gone on his merry way thrilling hoards of readers, while Michael Swanwick and Samuel Delaney... have not, if we are to judge by sheer numbers of readers. But if you've read *Stations of the Tide* and *Dhalgren*, you probably agree that Swanwick and Delaney do it *all* well, by any literary standard.

I can hear the helpful suggestions from mainstream readers already: *It's the covers. Those awful dragons depicted on fantasy books. Or those dreadful space ships.* Then there's the shelving issue—or where in the bookstore you might come across, say, *The Parable of the Talents* by Octavia Butler. To find Butler's Nebula award-winning book, you must venture into the slightly disreputable science fiction section and risk being seen in the company of ill-dressed thirteen-year-olds. And these are the *polite* reasons given by my friends who scorn science fiction and fantasy.

Some of these complaints about speculative fiction have merit, as I will show in a moment. Accusations of poor storytelling and sloppy prose, however, fall wide of the mark. Contrary to these too-simple explanations, I think Pullman's trilogy garnered its sales and rave reviews because of certain publishing and fictional choices unrelated to the quality of the writing. These choices removed barriers to the enjoyment of fantasy by the wider public. So, no, it wasn't solely the literary quality of His Dark Materials.

However, to convince the skeptical, I fear I must briefly rise to the defense of fantastic literature.

In Defense of the Fantastic

I am acutely aware that the Sorry State of Science Fiction and Fantasy is one that we in the industry have partially brought upon ourselves. We do set low literary standards for much of what we write and publish. Our covers depart from what most people find appealing. To make matters worse, the movies have defined us in their own, sadly superficial, terms. Filmmakers who use science fiction and fantasy concepts seem obsessed with digital special effects that are somehow guaranteed to recall science fiction's pulp origins—something long ago transcended by the best of our literature. To the Hollywood mentality, sophisticated content and subtlety will lose every battle with high tech dinosaurs and killer cyborgs.

I agree that some of the criticisms directed against speculative fiction are, if not actually deserved, at least understandable. Still, you have to admit that science fiction and fantasy do not stand alone in any lineup of criminally bad writing. A great deal of what we find in bookstores (never mind in supermarket racks) is pure drek. If I see another *Chicken Soup for Dummies* on the *New York Times* best seller list I'm going to make a scene at Borders. It needn't be in the Self Help section, either. The rarified precincts of the literary shelves are just as bad, chock full as they are with the self-consciously arty, stupefyingly dense and fashionably pointless. We *all* have our warts. If we are wearing tuxes, we may shoot our cuffs over them and say they are a virtue. But saying it over and over doesn't make it true.

A category should not be judged by its worst examples, I think we can agree. Among the recent best science fiction and fantasy writing you will find great stylists and luminous prose. Patricia McKillip is an example, along with William Gibson, Carol Emshwiller, China Mieville and A. A. Attanasio. If you've not read these authors, or take name familiarity as an endorsement, the names of Ray Bradbury and J. G. Ballard may help to drive home my point.

And if subversive concepts are your cup of tea, there can be no richer vein of strange and dissident ideas than in speculative fiction. This is what science fiction was born for, as witnessed by the iconic work of such greats as Philip K. Dick, Frank Herbert, Ursula Le Guin, Greg Bear and Michael Moorcock.

But despite these examples, fine work like Pullman's remains stubbornly aloof from the company of the rest of speculative fiction. The author of His Dark Materials colludes in this segregation. "I'm uneasy," Pullman said in an interview, "to think I write fantasy." Alas, fantasy. Perhaps we have not been welcoming to Mr. Pullman. Or perhaps he has toured the science fiction/fantasy stacks at a Crown Books superstore and drawn conclusions that are all too easy to draw. As I've said, it's partly our own fault that we don't put our best foot forward.

Maybe the time has come.

There's More Where That Came From

In spite of the unfair public aversion to speculative fiction, there lurks a saving grace. It is that those of you who loved the adventures of Lyra in His Dark Materials have some rare treats in store. There is more of Pullman's magic on the bookshelves—some of it not even by Philip Pullman.

I have a few books in mind that I think keep good company with *The Golden Compass, The Subtle Knife* and *The Amber Spyglass*. These are my quirky choices, and could as easily give way to other examples; however, my editor has forbidden a longer list. I will deftly avoid works by my friends—or people I owe money to. Here goes.

The Iron Dragon's Daughter by Michael Swanwick. This fantasy novel is a fun contrast to His Dark Materials. The protagonist, Jane, would surely be best friends with Pullman's Lyra, for they both are feisty youngsters without being insufferable, and merrily lie their way out of the iron fists of the church, villains and dragon factories. Published in 1993, Swanwick's story ends rather like Pullman's with a little girl assailing the Godhead in a hopeless gambit to end the suffering imposed by a cruel universe. In Swanwick's case, God is not a decrepit old man (since Darwin, traditional views of the Godhead aren't worth debunking in adult literature, perhaps) but a twisted geography of space-time given the cynical title of the Goddess. Young Jane straddles the many universes as does Lyra, and like Pullman's heroine, Jane is limited to just one at the end of the book. As brilliant and perverse as His Dark Materials, Swanwick's story gives us a wild tour of unbridled capitalism along with its garbage dumps and horrifying school traditions—all things we thought might be harmless—but not, we will learn—in Swanwick's hands.

Here are Elves tricked out in glamorous fashions, rust-belt factories eating the lives of indentured servants and shopping malls luring dwarves as well as the upwardly mobile. It is a story both wildly inventive and satisfyingly bound to Jane's coming-of-age story. This wonderful and atmospheric book goes on my coffee table. Yes, it has a green dragon depicted on the cover, but I remain unapologetic.

American Gods by Neil Gaiman. This is a contemporary urban fantasy, the winner of our genre's two highest awards. Similarities to His Dark Materials include masterful style, non-stop inventiveness and an appealing hero (Shadow, an Everyman, an ex-con) transformed at the end by sacrifice. Like Pullman, Gaiman takes on a huge theme and never flinches from it. In Gaiman's case, the topic is no less than the soul of America. Through the sometimes innocent eyes of Shadow, the reader takes a fantastical road trip through America where the old gods (Norse, Egyptian, African, Hindu) live out the remnants of their lives as con artists, undertakers and bums. Set against these powerful but faded mythologies are the "gods of credit cards and freeway, of Internet and telephone, of radio and hospital and television, gods of plastic and of beeper and of neon." What seems at first a mundane world is relentlessly undercut by Gaiman's magical landscapes of myth and heart. The reader drifts into acceptance of divine encounters, all the while yearning for something to believe in—something more than consumerism and celebrity. Freedom in America, the author has said, is "the freedom to believe the wrong thing, after all." Not that Gaiman preaches. Like most good subversive literature, the novel raises uncomfortable questions without forcing the answers. That Pullman *does* have answers, and pushes them rather hard, is the one aspect of his trilogy that bothers me.

American Gods is a dark book, like Pullman's. Why is this kind of story such a pleasure to read? I think it is because—despite what the mass media assume—we want to be disturbed as well as fascinated. *Been there, done that*, may be the laconic plea of our times—to encounter something of our world and ourselves that is new and deeper. At the end of *American Gods*, we have not found a new God. But Shadow finds, like Lyra, that after all the sacrifices, the human heart remains the only guide. I think this book will endure a very long time. Put it in your library next to *The Amber Spyglass*.

Thomas the Rhymer, by Ellen Kushner. Winner of the World Fantasy Award in 1991, this elegant tale of medieval love and the land of Faerie is no dreamy escapist fare, despite outward appearances. Yes, there is the historical figure of Thomas, and an agrarian and hierarchal society we've seen before in Tolkien and Robert Jordan. But after a grounding in the mundane world of bards and brigands we step with foreboding into a land of transformations and costly magics: the land of Faerie. In Kushner's dark and luminous tale everyone pays a heavy price for encounters with the Good Folk, none more so than our hero, whose lying, trickster ways are no match for the immortals, until love and pity move him to sacrifices he never dreamed he could offer. Even the powerful fairy queen is startled by acts of danger and integrity.

Side by side with His Dark Materials, *Thomas the Rhymer* provides equal pleasures: style, invention and storytelling. Its elegant prose, attempted by so many fantasies, lacks pretension and remains spare enough to suit a contemporary audience. As in Pullman's classic, we are privy to a lavish alternate world where the Elves discreetly drink blood, and the sport of the hunt hides terrible lusts and consequences. You will be kept guessing at the rules of the immortals' world, especially the queen's heart. As for the heart of the hero, this is always clear. Page by page Kushner lays bare the inner life of Thomas, in my opinion surpassing the characterization of Swanwick, Gaiman and Pullman.

So, no, you needn't check your mind at the door when you open works of fantasy. The likes of Neil Gaiman and Philip Pullman prove that magic, alien beings and alternate universes are no barrier to deep thought. In fact, in the hands of such practitioners, they invite it.

On the surface, this statement seems illogical. How can patently *made up* subject matter—far removed from ordinary experience—give us fresh insight? But it is precisely the strangeness of the material that allows passage of that jolt of understanding. When we lay aside disbelief in witches and Dust, the way is open to the ideas under the surface. We are vulnerable to open-mindedness. It is rather like putting on a mask or costume—a small matter at first—and, once at the party, putting on the personality to match. There's something intriguing about abandoning the stuffy garments of cultural norms. It's what science fiction and fantasy readers have always loved to do.

But did Philip Pullman do it better? Maybe so. After all, *he* is the one with the gazillion readers.

Skipping Past the Ghetto

Pullman certainly started out on the right foot. By publishing His Dark Materials as mainstream literature, he avoided being stereotyped as genre fantasy. No matter how lofty the stories of our best fantacists, it is common for all to be tarred with the same shoddy associations. As I've tried to illustrate, disdain of the genre is illogically, but indelibly, rooted. Because of this, Pullman's mainstream publication move made a lot of sense, as it did for J. K. Rowling.

Then there was the decision to write for young adults. Pullman saw the value in writing substantive literature for a younger audience. He has said that he wanted to tell a good story, and tell it in a straightforward way. He knew, however, that the literary establishment frowns on cogent narration. "The value of writing books for children," Pullman says, "is that they couldn't care less if you're Jeffrey Archer or Dostoyevsky. All they want to know is what happens next." As it happens—and here is where his trilogy begins to separate from the pack—a young audience will give you great latitude to play with strange (and dark) materials. Unsettling notions sit more easily on the shoulders of young people than on staid adults. Fantasy and young adults are a natural mix, as well as fantasy and children, as the Harry Potter books and The Chronicles of Narnia have proven. Young adults, after all, recently believed in magic and remember what it is like to take at face value the idea that priests can have *frogs* for souls.

As further evidence of the smart publishing strategy, consider the book covers. The publishers no doubt reasoned that with the right covers and positioning, parents might be tempted to pick up their kid's copy and have a look. Thus the gorgeous covers—with nary a fantastic element in view. The unwary adult picks up a good-looking book, never suspecting it is a fantasy. And even if they've heard it is a little offbeat (witches and magic doors), they can convince themselves that they're checking it out for the youngster on their gift list. But it is a false sense of safety. Like the Pied Piper of Hamlin, Pullman lures open-minded young adults down the road of dangerous ideas. Eagerly, they parade alongside him, while the adults follow a few steps behind.

We speculative fiction authors could follow Pullman too. But most of us remain stubbornly committed to adult literature. There are delights here that young adult fiction does not afford: more subtlety and complexity; grittiness and sometimes perversity. Whatever it is, most of us know when we're called upon to write for teenagers or children. Though it is a high calling, it remains a particular one.

But I don't mean to say that Philip Pullman has transcended the ghetto because of marketing strategy alone.

A Gentle Subversion

Pullman lowers us into subversive realms gently. Most fantasy and science fiction, however, plunge us there with a sudden click of ruby slippers. All well and good for devoted fans, but a bit too in-your-face for the less committed.

For example, Pullman's *The Golden Compass* begins in the wood-paneled library of a college much like Oxford, where we imagine ourselves safe from appalling ideas. (Well—there is the matter of the severed head in the box, but aside from that, we feel assured.) A book for young adults, how nice. The cover is gorgeous, depicting a child and a cuddly polar bear. All very civilized and appealing. But toward the end of the second book in the series we are rooting for witches and hoping that God will die of an aneurism before the nice little boy has to put him out of his rotten misery with a quick jab of the subtle knife. We seethe with indignation: How could this so-called God doom billions of the dead to a horrifying underworld that forcibly exiles them from their own souls, for crying out loud? Kill the Old Man, put Him out of His misery.

Well, yes. But how did we get from Oxford to hating God? Slowly, for one thing. *The Golden Compass* begins:

> Lyra and her dæmon moved through the darkening hall, taking care to keep to one side, out of sight of the kitchen. The three great tables that ran the length of the hall were laid already, the silver and the glass catching what little light there was, and the long benches were pulled out ready for the guests. Portraits of former Masters hung high up in the gloom along the walls. Lyra reached the dais and looked back at the open kitchen door, and, seeing no one, stepped up beside the high table. The places here were laid with gold, not silver, and the fourteen seats were not oak benches but mahogany chairs with velvet cushions.

How different is Pullman's opening from Swanwick's *The Iron Dragon's Daughter*:

> The changeling's decision to steal a dragon and escape was born, though she did not know it then, the night the children met to plot the death of their supervisor.
>
> She had lived in the steam dragon plant for as long as she could remember. Each dawn she was marched with other indentured minors from their dormitory in Building 5 to the cafeteria for a breakfast she barely had time to choke down before work. Usually she was then sent to the cylinder machine shop for polishing labor, but other times she was assigned to Building 12 where the black iron bodies were inspected and oiled before being sent to the erection shop for final assembly. The abdominal tunnels were too small for an adult. It was her duty to crawl within them to swab out and then grease those dark passages.

She worked until sunset and sometimes later if there was a particularly important dragon under contract.

Her name was Jane.

Swanwick brings us immediately into a child-exploiting Dickensian factory, oddly geared to the making of metal dragons. This is a lot to absorb in two paragraphs. *Weird*, the mainstream reader may think, his step already slowing as he looks up as though hoping for a cab out of a bad neighborhood.

In contrast, Pullman opens his story with a setting which at first seems much like our own world. A college, scholars, butlers, curious little girls and poison wine. Then come the slight alterations: animal familiars, "philosophical instruments," cities dimly seen in the sky and the glowing particles of a mysterious substance called Dust. Within the first two chapters we take our first halting steps into the realm of His Dark Materials. Here, Pullman twists reality so slowly that unwary readers are fully committed to the story by the time they are jumping from one universe to the next through little doors in the air cut open by the subtle knife.

I think Pullman is on to something here.

If writers of fantastic literature desired a wider audience, we could do worse than remember that a sought-after storyteller is deceptively gentle. At first.

Of Dust and Dæmons

In orchestrating a new realm of reality, Pullman is using a tried and true technique of fantastic literature known as *distancing*, to borrow Ursula Le Guin's term from her essay "Why Americans are Afraid of Dragons." With this approach, an author creates a bit of psychological distance between the material and the reader. The writer creates an alien or magical land where the reader doesn't at first recognize the intellectual landscape. Thus challenging ideas are introduced *in new environments*, where we feel buffered from the impacts of these ideas. We are not forced to directly challenge our cherished beliefs. Many of us resist stories that promise to do so. However, in new environments, we may not recognize that these beliefs are actually our own; they belong, supposedly, to elves or witches or aliens.

In distancing, an author uses a little sleight of hand to say, "don't reject this just now; wait awhile; perhaps these bizarre things are true here, but nowhere else." And later, when you begin to suspect that your favorite ideas are being skewered, the author, hiding behind a cohesive and interesting story, whispers: "It's only a story. Let's just see what happens next, shall we?" The fictional purpose is that, by giving us some psychological distance from the real world, we more fully participate in the story.

This is terribly important. It has been said that stories "happen" in the space between the author's words and the reader's mind. Readers help tell the story by bringing their own experience to the page. If so, then the one thing a writer wants to avoid is "bumping" the reader out of the story. We want to engage the reader as fully as possible.

It may seem odd to call such bonding "distancing." But its very value lies in a suspension of disbelief just long enough to get past adult-bred blockages and stuffiness. We must accept Dust and dæmons. At the other end of the book, having traveled far, we are able to see Lyra as the new Eve and applaud her first kiss with Will as not merely an inevitable romance, but a triumph of the heart.

Similarly, using distancing, Ursula Le Guin in *The Left Hand of Darkness* brings me as a reader to question how much I am defined by my gender, and to wonder what culture could arise where there *was* no absolute gender. Michael Moorcock in *Gloriana* confronts me with the price of empire, the inevitable corruption that accompanies orthodox power. And Michael Swanwick, in *The Iron Dragon's Daughter*, reveals that Western popular culture is as worthy a ground of suffering as Middle Earth or Macbeth's Inverness. I might not have *wanted* to think so, but now I am, if not convinced, at least deepened by the provocative thought.

I have taken a twisty but rewarding path to a full appreciation of Philip Pullman's trilogy. He's not just a lucky devil who struck the right chord with the reading public—he wrote a substantial fantasy story that broke the barriers, not of literature, but of people.

I don't expect a huge Pullmanian audience for science fiction and fantasy any time soon. By the standards of wide readership and literary attention, fantastic literature has, for the most part, missed the boat. Like jazz and sushi, speculative fiction will remain an acquired taste. That's all right. I think I know why: The covers. A neighborhood with a bad reputation. The off chance that one might shed one's clothes and cavort with unsavory characters.

Denied the mantle of respectability, we science fiction and fantasy writers may look wistfully on Pullman's success, but that won't stop us from enjoying His Dark Materials even more, perhaps, than most readers do. After all, it's kindred literature. Besides, there are lessons to be learned from Philip Pullman—and vice versa, of course.

I've learned one lesson for sure: Catching a glimpse of *The Golden Compass* on my neighbor's coffee table, I am not deceived when she says, "My nephew just loves it." I nod and smile. But I know what's really going on.

She's reading fantastic literature under the covers, by flashlight.

Kay Kenyon's science fiction novels include The Seeds of Time, Maximum Ice *and* The Braided World; *the latter two were finalists for the Philip K. Dick and John W. Campbell awards, respectively. Her speculative fiction explores themes such as cultural and biological transformation and the dilemmas presented by alien contact. She has recently completed her most challenging novel to date,* Bright of the Sky, *the first of a quartet of books.*

O, To Be in Oxford...

I want to ride through the night on an armored polar bear! I want to cut holes in the air and step through into other worlds! I want to fly in an airship over the Arctic snow! But most of all, I want to live like Lyra as a kid in her alternative Oxford!

What a life! Running on the rooftops, spitting plumstones onto the heads of passersby, engaging in alliances and wars, pelting the enemy with clods of earth! Or exploring underground cellars, drinking forbidden wine! Best of all—*no parents!*

Let's face it. What's the worst thing about being a kid in this non-alternative present-day reality of ours? It's the way parents and adults want to involve themselves in your life, right? It's the *surveillance.* Loving surveillance, caring surveillance—but still surveillance. Someone is always worrying themselves sick over you. If it's not parents, it's all the other adults. Medical specialists worry about your weight and diet, educators worry about your behavior and brain and TV chat shows worry that you're taking drugs. For anything you do, there's always someone checking up on whether it's harmful or beneficial to your future development. In every moment of your life, you're the center of attention. The curse of perpetual *importance!*

Lucky, lucky Lyra! You aren't important at all. In place of biological parents, you have the scholars of Jordan College as your stand-in fathers, and *they* wouldn't know a childhood game if it whacked them on the head. They're well-intentioned and kindly enough, but their minds are far far away in the clouds of experimental theology. Your only stand-in mother is Mrs. Lonsdale, the briskly impatient housekeeper who has no time and hardly any affection to expend on a mere *child.*

No, not important at all...and that also goes for society at large. In your alternative Victorian reality, children are given a very small walk-on sit-down don't-fidget role in adult society. "Speak when you're spoken to, be quiet and polite, smile nicely and don't you ever say *Dunno* when someone asks you a question," Mrs. Lonsdale tells Lyra in *The Golden Compass*. Children don't feature as children, only as adults would like to see them. No mutual sharing or exchange in this society! "No grown-up ever gave reasons of their own accord," thinks Lyra (TGC p.56)

How can this be good? Well, ignorance cuts both ways. If grown-ups don't level with kids, then the kids don't have to level with grown-ups. Lyra and her friends have their own world that the adults never even know about. Picture Lyra in our reality—she'd never get away with any of her tricks. Kids forming up gangs, roaming around unsupervised? Shock! Horror! Lyra and her friends would be a *social problem*. Psychiatrists would be called upon to provide deep explanations, social workers would get their knickers in a terrible twist. Unsound behavior leading to habitual stealing (how Lyra loves a good theft, anything from apples to horse-rides!). As for clambering around on rooftops—there would be a public outcry! So dangerous for the poor little dears, so many dreadful accidents just waiting to happen! What can the parents or guardians be thinking of? Utter irresponsibility! Quick, bring them down from their game and put them in a risk-free playground, with nice low ladders and bars. Better still, drive them to supervised sport, supervised swimming lessons, dancing lessons, supervised anything!

Oh Lyra, you have a freedom that a kid could hardly dream of nowadays. Instead of designer playgrounds, you have your special secret territory in the leftover corners of the adult world. Up on the roofs, you rule a realm that no adult shares, an extended country with its own zones and routes and accesses. So close to their territory, but forgotten, unnoticed! And down underground, a vast hidden wasteland of cellars waiting for exploration. No adult ever went ahead and prepared it for you, pre-planning what you'd see and how you'd play. You live in a parallel universe that makes only passing contact with the adult universe. Out of sight and out of mind! You don't have to fight to keep your secrets to yourself. The adults aren't even interested!

Did I mention the gang warfare? Your warfaring activities are as invisible to adults as all the other important things in your life.

Just as [Lyra] was unaware of the hidden currents of politics running below the surface of College affairs, so the Scholars, for their part, would have been unable to see the rich seething stew of alliances and enmities and feuds and treaties which was a child's life in Oxford. Children playing together: how pleasant to see! What could be more innocent and charming?

In fact, Lyra and her peers were engaged in deadly warfare. There were several wars running at once.

There's that word "rich" again. Your world may be small in scope, but it has all the complexities of full-scale international affairs. Sides fluctuate all the time: college versus college, collegers versus townies, collegers and townies versus the brickburners' children, *everyone* versus the gyptians... the only constant is that the rivalries are "deep and satisfying." How you enjoy the "endless opportunities for provoking warfare"!

Tut-tut-tut! I can imagine the murmur of disapproval in our non-alternative present-day reality. Surely this is *very incorrect* behavior! Children aren't supposed to be this way, or if they are, they must have been influenced by the adults' bad example. *Tut! Tut!* Such behavior should be discouraged. Not by obvious harsh punishment, of course—but by endless grinding pressure: *Think of others, be considerate, how would you like to be hit by a flying clod of earth?* Until, in the end, all the fun would have been sucked out of the game. The kids might not have learned to be gentle, but they'd have learned to feel guilty.

None of that endless grinding pressure for you, Lyra! You're more likely to get a smack, as Mrs. Lonsdale gives you a smack, only because your knees are dirty. If you're caught hiding in the Retiring Room, you expect to be severely punished. For minor misdemeanors, you'll probably have to endure a stern lecture. But so what? You don't make a fuss, you answer humbly or you look at the floor and hold your tongue. In five minutes, it'll be over and you can get back to your own life again. Who can't put up with a bad five minutes?

I suppose that's why you don't bother to harbor resentments. The adults don't understand you—but that goes without saying. At least they don't lodge inside your head with sneaky little voices that keep telling you how *they* think you ought to behave. These adults are simple, external forces: when they're not there, they're not there. They belong to a different species—like rhinos. The most they can do is flatten you. No point being sullen or holding a grudge; you just stay out of their way. As for what goes on in their minds—who cares? They're only adults, only rhinos!

That's the trouble in our non-alternative present-day reality. Secretly or not so secretly, the adults are more than half in love with childhood;

they long to share and recapture it for themselves. But sorry, olds; it won't work! The moment an adult gets involved, childhood is no longer childhood. It's like the scientist and the electron—you can't observe without changing the nature of what you observe. For "scientist" read "adult," for "electron" read "child." Heisenberg would have understood.

What Lyra and her friends have created is a separate kids' culture. It may be brutal, as when Lyra and Roger roast and eat a rook. Even Pullman describes Lyra as a barbarian, a coarse and greedy little savage. In *The Golden Compass* Iorek slices open a seal and Lyra digs out its kidneys and loves the taste of them raw. But is this so very different to, say, Lapp culture?

Lyra's way of life may look uncivilized to an outside observer, just as so-called "primitive" tribes may look uncivilized to a Western visitor. But in fact, "primitive" tribes have incredibly complex systems of belief and social organization—ask any anthropologist. Same with Lyra and her friends: they have very elaborate codes and games and hierarchies. The standards are different but the complexities are on a par. This isn't a junior version of adult culture, but a fully evolved culture on its own.

How long would such a culture survive in our non-alternative present-day reality? Just imagine! As soon as any new interest evolved, the adult world of commerce and marketing would instantly suck it up. I can already see the glitzy cellophane-wrapped boxes:

THE ROOFTOP GAME! Improved board game version! Twice the excitement and none of the danger!

Or what about:

COLLEGERS VS TOWNIES, the all-new electronic war game! Hours of endless fun! The kids will love it! Only $59.95!

That's what I mean—everything gets taken over. The toy companies find out what the kids like, insert themselves into the loop and turn kids' games into commodities. Their games are taken over and sold back to them, glamorized with bells and whistles. Of course the kids are seduced! But what they've lost is their own separate culture. Now they have only a mixed and mushy culture, half-and-half.

There's a half-and-half culture in *The Golden Compass,* though not the children's culture: the polar bears of Svalbard. In the past, the bears had been happy with their traditional way of life, valuing their armor and their honor, never missing the company of a dæmon. Under Iofur Raknison, however, they fell under the glamorized influence of human culture. Now they want dæmons of their own—so they make little dolls for themselves and pretend to talk to them. Poor sad polar bears! Now their way of life is founded on lies and doublethink. They're divided in culture and divided in themselves, neither fish nor fowl, neither one thing nor the other.

By contrast, the kids' culture in *The Golden Compass* is self-consistent and self-contained. They can even create a new game to incorporate the threat of the Gobblers. "Let's play kids and Gobblers," Lyra suggests to Roger. Unprotected by adults, Lyra and her friends have to deal with dangers in their own terms.

It's because her own culture is so strong and rich that Lyra can resist the lure of the adult world, as represented by Mrs. Coulter. Yes, for a while Lyra is seduced when Mrs. Coulter carries her off to London, showers her with presents, dazzles her with sophistication and flatters her with attention. It's the oldest trick in the book, pretending to be Lyra's equal and her friend! But Lyra doesn't stay seduced for long. Even before discovering Mrs. Coulter's true nature in *The Golden Compass* she starts to get bored:

> She had been feeling confined and cramped by this polite life, however luxurious it was. She would have given anything for a day with Roger and her Oxford ragamuffin friends, with a battle in the claybeds and a race along the canal.

Lyra has her own world elsewhere, which is where she belongs. No amount of attention or glamour can compete with that.

But if you've been given attention from a very early age...attention is the key to it all. This is how I see it: in our non-alternative reality, we're drip-fed with attention all through childhood until we get hooked on it. Attention becomes a drug, the only thing that makes us feel we exist. We can't do without it. But as attention-seekers, we're helplessly dependent upon attention-givers. Sure, we talk about doing our own thing, being our own person—but we have to have other people watching us do it! Our lives are dominated by the need for more and more attention!

Richard Harland lives between the golden beaches and green hills of Wollongong, south of Sydney in Australia. For ten years, he was a university academic, with three published books on the philosophy of language. Then he resigned to become a full-time writer. He has published sf thrillers (the Eddon and Vail series), a fantasy trilogy (the Ferren books) and two gothic cult novels. His latest novel, The Black Crusade, won the Aurealis Award for Best Horror Novel of 2004 and the Golden Aurealis Award for Best Novel in any category of sf, fantasy or horror.

GREGORY MAGUIRE

Pull Up a Chair

This piece first appeared in *The Horn Book Magazine* in 2000.

Armed with a rare numbered typescript copy of *The Amber Spyglass*, I'm tempted to roll up my shirtsleeves, light a cigar, splash some Tokay into a glass and discuss fine points of reason, fancy and theology before all hell breaks loose—an amusement that, with the publication of the unsettling third volume of His Dark Materials, just may come to pass. Perhaps my yielding to the temptation of a theological colloquy wouldn't be an unsuitable reaction to *The Amber Spyglass*. The nature of temptation is one of the book's most compelling if less explicit themes.

But, readers, here's a temptation for you. I find it impossible to consider this serious novel without revealing some of its secrets. So if you want to enjoy your first experience of this long-awaited fantasy thriller as a virgin reader, innocent of my plot synopses or interpretations, flag this review and come back to it later.

So: Finally we have the much-awaited conclusion to the trilogy. Adorned with its devastating cover art by Eric Rohmann, *The Amber Spyglass* delivers much of what was promised in the preceding cliffhangers, *The Golden Compass* and *The Subtle Knife*. (If you need a refresher, you couldn't do better than to listen to the unparalleled audio recordings of each, available from Random House/Listening Library.) Most of the characters from the earlier books, beloved or bedeviled or both, return to continue their fateful roles in this saga that capsizes—or apocalypsizes—the Book of Genesis for our secular humanist times.

Lyra Belacqua and Will Parry, last seen beyond Alamo Gulch in one world or another, are set to escape from the clutches of Lyra's mother, the fiendish and prevaricating Mrs. Coulter. (For my money Mrs. Coulter beats out the panserbjorne and dæmons as Pullman's most delicious invention, since Mrs. Coulter is the least predictable among Pullman's dramatis personae.) The book rollicks and careers with the narrative gale force we've come to expect. Philip Pullman achieves effects that rival the best accomplishments of the earlier books. In any given chapter Pullman offers more sensuous description and narrative brio than are found in most entire novels. A plot summary can sound breathless and ridiculous, but, friends, it can't be helped. When a novel takes place in multiple worlds, a lot of happenings happen.

In freeing Lyra from the clutches of her mother, Will breaks and helps repair the subtle knife. Lyra, burdened by her accidental betrayal of Roger the kitchen boy, persuades Will to join her in hunting for Roger's ghost in the land of the dead, whose Stygian murk has never been so fully and hauntingly described. (The book's strongest scenes are here, as the children wrestle with chthonic mysteries and sacrifice much to liberate Limbo or its like.) On their emergence from the underworld, the children find that the long-awaited battle with Heaven is about to be joined. Assisted by bears, witches, ghosts and airborne chevaliers from yet another world, the rebel angels make a better go of it this time. The regent of Heaven is the angel Metatron (a name derived from Greek roots that, put together this way, suggest a higher or late-model elementary particle). He is overthrown at last, dashed down into a pit that makes Malebolge in Dante's *Inferno* look like leafy suburban sprawl. Oh, and by the way, God dies.

Finally the pace slackens, and with relief we are swept into the sweet temptation and succumbing of Lyra and Will. Yes, the ur-couple of a million million universes falls in love. We can draw the inference that, as the Old Testament might have put it, Will and Lyra come to know each other, though this is discreetly handled and open to interpretation, both textual and theological. The final chapter is all the more wrenching because until now poignancy has not seemed one of Pullman's strengths.

I'm amazed and relieved to report that the author pulls off most of what he attempts, though I feel the need for more vast depths of time than I have so I might reread the completed saga at once. I want to organize all these worlds in my mind. I want to test the implications of the theology to make sure that they are supported by the contortions of the plot. I trust that many readers, young and old, are going to be left with magnificent questions. The big ones. And why not? That's what books are for.

So put another log on the fire and draw your chairs closer and tell me. Is this a book about the death of God or about the defeat of an institutionalized authority unsupported by moral credibility? Can there be such a thing as temptation in a world in which sin has lost its meaning? Is there a creator of all things? The Ancient of Days, unceremoniously spilled from His carriage (caps on the possessive pronoun mine, by lifelong habit), is God but seems not to be the creator; whence, then, did He get His authority? Even in a fantasy, can God be something other than, as Saint Thomas Aquinas defined, "that which all men agree to call God"? Can a novel truly be about religion if spirituality is no more than a physical phenomenon—angels, dæmons, Dust? With the concept of prophecy (as pertains to Lyra particularly) implying predestination, who organized destiny in a universe wherein God is supposed to be senile and ineffectual? Who, or what, propels prophetic fate? And if "the Christian religion is a very powerful and convincing mistake," as a sympathetic character remarks, what are Buddhists and Ismailis and Jains and even soft-tongued Quakers to make of His Dark Materials?

And what is the nature of Dust, really? Do we know? It had seemed to be an aura that surrounds maturing human beings and the artifacts wrought by human consciousness. But in *The Amber Spyglass* the nature of Dust seems subtly expanded; it now seems related to every physical aspect of every world, including natural forces like wind and the moon, which are exempt from human interference. I'm not sure even now that I would know Dust if I saw it, even with an amber spyglass, the tool Mary Malone uses to examine Dust's traffic patterns.

As the ambitious series approaches its worlds-shaking conclusions, I sense that despite clear philosophical antipathies, Pullman draws closer to and perhaps derives more from C. S. Lewis' Space Trilogy than from the works of Tolkien or Susan Cooper, to whom he has been compared. And Pullman shares a lot with Lewis: a moral ferocity, albeit of a very different order; a bravura ability to conceive and set in motion a huge narrative apparatus; a knack for the invention of species and worlds. (You'll love the Mulefa.) Fusty old Narnia looks awfully tame, even somewhat Disneyfied, by comparison.

I suspect it will take all of us a while to discern the counterpoints and the overtones in this massive symphonic accomplishment. I confess my own moral compass is probably more tarnished brass than gold, my critical knife less than subtle; with my spiritual spyglass I still see through a glass darkly, not through amber. But for the sake of ringing out news about this book I struggle for magnificent metaphors and appropriate adjectives. Pour me some more Tokay and let's see what we have.

How shall we call it? In the end, His Dark Materials is not Shakespearian because, the divinely complicated Mrs. Coulter aside, Pullman's characters seem to exist in the grip of their fate rather than in defiance of it. Nor can the trilogy properly be called Miltonic, despite the subject matter—the rebel angels battling over *Paradise Lost*. Milton's work, after all, no matter how it gets away from him, is driven by devotion. And though it sure rockets along, His Dark Materials is nonetheless not Spielbergian, for (like the J. K. Rowling Pullman must know he'll be compared to) Steven Spielberg is at heart a Gothicist, and Pullman avoids dread for its own sake. Perhaps the books are more akin to the Enlightenment labors of a Rousseau and a Descartes, even a Defoe. Pullman sets himself a nigh-impossible challenge: to construct an apologia for secular rationality in the form of a fantasy, which is a most seductive and pleasingly irrational form of literature.

In the end, with the mysteries of dark matter resolved, we have only the mysteries of our own dark human selves to contemplate. We close the book with a sigh of elegiac parting. The bears are back tempering steel for their armor, the witches flying about on branches of cloud pine, forging new alliances. Bereft of fantasy and, perhaps, faith, we mortals must resume tempering our hopes for fulfillment and fleeing our fears of disenchantment, twin tasks that circumscribe our days.

Many readers will put down *The Amber Spyglass* only to pick up *The Golden Compass* again and begin anew, to see how it all fits. But it may not matter how often one goes back to the earlier books. As Pullman says of God's demise, we may only find "a mystery dissolving in mystery." Is this not a workable definition of the sacred? Well, whether Dust is defined or not, in a certain garden Lyra and Will, like all of us, are left alone with the unresolvable question framed best, perhaps, by Shakespeare, from Sonnet LIII:

What is your substance, whereof are you made, That millions strange shadows on you tend?

Turn the light out as you leave. I'll sit here in the dark and think a little while longer.

Gregory Maguire is co-director of Children's Literature New England, Incorporated, and author of books for children and adults, including Wicked: The Life and Times of the Wicked Witch of the West *and* Son of a Witch.

Occam's Razor and *The Subtle Knife*
Invention in His Dark Materials

Philip Pullman's His Dark Materials is one of the more remarkable young adult fantasy trilogies of the past generation. The first book, *The Golden Compass*, has to be the best YA Robert A. Heinlein or Ursula K. Le Guin never wrote. At the climax of the third, *The Amber Spyglass*, God dies, and we don't miss Him a bit when He's gone.

There's a lot of ground to cover from the altered Oxford of the first book to the altered multiverse of the last. There are a lot of high points to hit, and some potholes, too. Let's take a look at what went right...and also at some of the things that may make a reader raise an eyebrow or two.

The Golden Compass has more in common with Heinlein than with Le Guin. Lyra Belacqua's world is intricately realized, and the plot revolves around scientific puzzles. The sciences involved, however, more closely resemble what would be sorcery in our normal, mundane world.

Even human nature—or rather, the way human nature is expressed in the created world. *The Golden Compass* opens, "Lyra and her dæmon moved through the darkening hall, taking care to keep to one side, out of sight of the kitchen." Dæmons are external manifestations of the spirit. Lyra's dæmon, Pantalaimon, is her scout, her advisor, her confidant—literally, her other self.

And Lyra needs all those things, because she is, to put it mildly, high-spirited and adventurous. She and Heinlein's Podkayne Fries would get on well; if they ever found themselves in the same universe, they would bring it to its knees in nothing flat. She is a delightful character; watching her go again and again where she isn't supposed to and watching her grow by doing so are two intertwined pleasures.

Her father, Lord Asriel, is frequently absent. Her mother, Mrs. Coulter, is even more frequently alarming, as is the older woman's dæmon, a golden monkey. (My youngest daughter, a volunteer at the Los Angeles Zoo, says she can't look at golden lion tamarins the way she would if she'd never read the trilogy.)

Ordinary humans share the world of *The Golden Compass* with iron-working bears who live in the far north. The combat between the bear Iofur Raknison, corrupted by human ways, and the exiled Iorek Byrnison, a bruin of the old school, for the kingship is one of the great adventure scenes in fantastic literature, and the cry, *"Bears! Who is your king?"* at the end will make even a mere human's hackles rise.

Guided by her alethiometer (Greek for "truth measurer"—think of it as a Ouija board on steroids), Lyra travels north still in her world, and at the end of *The Golden Compass* crosses from her universe into another, where she meets Will Parry, who is from our world.

The Subtle Knife, the middle book of His Dark Materials, suffers the problem typical of middle books of trilogies, one that can be summed up in four words: beginning, muddle and end. Things are going on, but there is no real resolution; if there were a full resolution at the end of the second book, we wouldn't have a trilogy.

And *The Subtle Knife* suffers in another way when compared to *The Golden Compass*: we see most of it from Will's point of view, and he is less interesting than Lyra. Lyra is always sure of herself—not always right, but always sure. Her energy and persistence make everything and everyone around her come alive. Will often hasn't the faintest idea what to do, and has to be forced into action. Once forced, he is effective, but a character who acts from volition rather than compulsion will grab more readers than the other kind.

Once he gets his hand on the subtle knife—the title MacGuffin of the second book, as the alethiometer is of the first (at least in its American incarnation; the British title is *Northern Lights*), things become vastly more complicated. The knife can—subtly—cut paths between the universes. One of these is inhabited by Specters that batten on the spiritual energy of adults—and that threaten to get into other universes through the rents the subtle knife has already made between them.

One universe, two universes, a few universes...all of which are setup for *The Amber Spyglass*, in which, as Cole Porter puts it, anything goes. We find ourselves in a universe inhabited by Mulefa, intelligent creatures with wheels and trunks who are, though technologically back-ward, much nicer than most humans. Lyra and Will also make the ac-quaintance of the Gallivespians, tiny humanlike spies who travel by gi-ant dragonflies and are armed with poison spurs on their heels.

And there are angels, a journey through hell and a great many other marvels, the aforementioned death of God and a happy ending after that. Even though *The Amber Spyglass* is a good deal longer than either *The Golden Compass* or *The Subtle Knife*, this is a lot to ask of any book. The general impression created is rather like that of the German ar-mored cruisers—the "pocket battleships"—of World War II: very pow-erful guns and strong armor on a hull without enough displacement to do them justice.

One of the—many—joys of *The Golden Compass* is the worldbuild-ing. This is some of the most excellent and convincing yet unobtrusive work anyone has ever done. From the Oxford rooftops to the boats of the gyptians on the canals (the gyptians, of course, are gypsies, both names arising from the mistaken belief that the people arose in Egypt) to the horrors of the laboratory where kidnapped children have their dæmons amputated to the bears' town on the northern island of Svalbard....Nothing seems ad hoc. Nothing seems contrived. Every-thing rings true. Building a world, and doing so without breaking out in expository lumps, is one of the hardest challenges facing any writer of speculative fiction, and *The Golden Compass* is not merely a success but a tour de force.

Part of the reason everything here works so well, I think, is that for much of the book Pullman is writing and altering what he knows well. He attended this universe's Oxford, and is intimately familiar with the university and the surrounding town. This gives him an enormous head start in transposing a familiar song to an unfamiliar key, as it were. Here I speak from experience; in creating the magic-powered Los Angeles of *The Case of the Toxic Spell Dump*, I chose to focus on and modify areas where I'd really lived. Some of the people with whom my protagonist works are based on people I'd worked with myself, and the bureaucratic finagling and office politics of the fictional Environmental Perfection Agency mirror those of the real (and occasionally surreal) Los Angeles County Office of Education. It's much easier to make something feel real when you're basing it on something that *is* real.

Just how high Pullman sets the bar for himself in the first book of His Dark Materials he proceeds to illustrate in the next two. The main interest in *The Subtle Knife* should be the clash of universes and world views—expressed in character terms, of course—between the lovingly imagined alternate world of *The Golden Compass* and the mundane Oxford that Will inhabits and Lyra eventually reaches.

We see some of that, but not enough. Lyra takes too much for granted—not least the strangeness of a place where people's spirits live inside their heads, rather than as externally manifested dæmons—and her arrival and actions in our world feel more rushed and arbitrary than they should. The Cittàgazze of yet another world and the subsequent chase through others have this slightly insubstantial feel, as if they are the way they are for no better reason than that the author requires them to be so.

If these places are based on things Pullman has seen and experienced for himself, it doesn't show. One of the things that makes Tolkien's *The Lord of the Rings* so persuasive is the feeling he gives that the geography of his created world exists independently of his characters and predates them. The mountains and the Dwarves' caverns and the Dead Marshes seem to have been there before Frodo had to slog through them, and would have been there just the same if he hadn't come along. Pullman's Oxford has this same aura of inevitability to it. The new worlds revealed—perhaps too briefly revealed—in *The Subtle Knife* don't.

This trend of almost excessive inventiveness continues and accelerates in *The Amber Spyglass*. As long ago as 1902, H. G. Wells observed, "The thing that makes such imaginations interesting is their translation into commonplace terms and a rigid exclusion of other marvels from the story. Then it becomes human. How would you feel and what might not happen to you, is the typical question, if for instance pigs could fly and one came rocketing over a hedge at you? How would you feel and what might not happen if suddenly you were changed into an ass and couldn't tell anyone about it? Or if you suddenly became invisible? But no one would think twice about the answer if hedges and houses also began to fly, or if people changed into lions, tigers, cats and dogs left and right, or if anyone could vanish anyhow. Nothing remains interesting where anything might happen."

Wells' wise dictum is a literary restatement of an important philosophical principle often termed Occam's Razor. William of Occam (died c. 1349) wrote, "*Essentia non sunt multiplicanda praeter necessitatem*": elements are not to be multiplied except when necessary. In other words, when faced with two conflicting possibilities, choose the simpler unless you have some very good reason not to do so.

This, throughout the last two books of His Dark Materials, is precisely what Philip Pullman fails to do. He continually introduces universes and ideas that not only do not exist in *The Golden Compass* but do not seem to be imagined or anticipated there. It is as if, in *The Golden Compass*, he is playing with an ordinary deck of cards, while in *The Subtle Knife* and *The Amber Spyglass* he adds the Major Arcana from the tarot deck. It's not that such decks haven't been around at least as long as the more common sort. But, if we don't have some hints earlier on that we are likely to see cards from them, introducing such cards does make us wonder about the rules of the game.

Take the Gallivespians, for instance. What are they? They are plot contrivances. They are gallant, swaggering, poison-heeled plot contrivances flitting about on their dragonfly steeds' gossamer wings, but they are plot contrivances nonetheless. If we need to find out what the bad guys are up to but can't plausibly put another good guy at their meeting, what do we do? We use a Gallivespian.

Besides serving as plot contrivances, Gallivespians also seem to be highly improbable. They are of human proportions and human intelligence, but no more than a handspan high—say, about eight inches. If a Gallivespian is 1/8 as tall as a man, his brain will only be about 1/512 the size of a man's. This does not leave a lot of room for thought, a problem Pullman unfortunately fails to consider.

Gallivespians are contrived in yet another way: nothing in the previous two books prepares us for their existence or for their introduction in *The Amber Spyglass*. We have been led to believe that the worlds through which our characters travel are more similar to one another than eventually proves the case.

In an introductory note, Pullman himself writes, "*The Golden Compass* forms the first part of a story in three volumes. The first volume is set in a universe like ours, but different in many ways. The second volume begins in the universe we know, and then it and the third volume will move between the universes."

Pullman is an admirable writer in ever so many ways. No one, I think, would deny that one of the admirable qualities he displays is precision. In this introductory note, he mentions only two universes: Lyra's and ours. *Between* is a conjunction that normally links two things and two things only. He gets even more specific; he says the second and third books will move between *the* universes. Again, the almost inevitable inference the reader draws is that Lyra's universe and our own are the only two in this created cosmos.

And that turns out not to be so. Does it ever!

Had Pullman said, "then it and the third volume will move among universes," we would be warned that what we see in *The Golden Compass* isn't everything we'll get. Since he doesn't, we are taken by surprise, and in a less pleasant way than we might like. *There are more things in heaven and earth, Horatio, / Than are dreamt of in your philosophy.* Fair enough. But things presented as true in the third book of a trilogy should at least be dreamt of in the first one.

Objections similar to those raised about the Gallivespians also apply to the Mulefa. They are interesting, they are alien and their properties seem more calculated to advance the story than to make them convincing on their own. Creatures that depend on wheels are improbable—to put it mildly—in evolutionary terms. Mary Malone, who is transported to their world, notes this and notes their dependence on the seed pods that let them move so well—but there is no attempt to explain how such an unusual symbiosis came to be. It is simply presented as a fait accompli, which makes it feel less probable than it might otherwise. Pullman's creation seems stronger when it stays closer to more traditional models.

Science fiction and fantasy have dealt with the death of God before. Two examples that spring to mind are James Blish's *Black Easter*, a genuinely terrifying and terrifyingly believable novel, and James Morrow's *Towing Jehovah*, perhaps the blackest black comedy ever written. Philip Pullman may be the first sf writer to deal with this them at the YA level, however.

It's ironic that the Harry Potter books should have drawn so much fire from fundamentalist groups, while His Dark Materials seems to have largely sneaked under their radar. Yes, the Potter novels have magic and witchcraft and wizardry and dæmons and other things spooky and supernatural. But they are at bottom profoundly respectful of authority and convention. Yes, there is a different power hierarchy, but the hierarchy is still there, whether it springs from the muggles' City Hall or from the Ministry of Magic. And you can bet your bottom fifty pence that when J. K. Rowling finishes the series, Harry Potter will find and accept his assigned role in his social structure and the bad guys will get what's coming to them.

His Dark Materials is much less friendly to the powers that be. It is, in fact, profoundly subversive—not surprising, when the trilogy takes its title from God's leftovers in *Paradise Lost*, through which Satan sets out to journey. The lesson Pullman teaches is that God is old, ancient, senile and irrelevant to the universe as it is these days; that when He dies the worlds just keep going on as they always have, and that we have to measure things by themselves and in their own context, not against Him. Why the people who hate and fear J. K. Rowling's work aren't calling for burning Pullman at the stake or crucifying him, who can say? But they don't seem to be.

Again, the only thing wrong with anything in *The Amber Spyglass* is that it doesn't seem to arise from what came before it. His Dark Materials is a hippogriff of a trilogy—lion, eagle and horse uneasily pasted together—where it should have been an organic whole. One wonders whether Pullman was really sure where he was going when he started on his journey and started Lyra on hers. Did he plan from the beginning to have her go from Oxford to hell? If he did, he might have offered us a few more clues earlier on about the nature of the road she was taking: we might have seen angels sooner, for instance. Without adequate foreshadowing, we sometimes feel dragged along rather than smoothly guided.

And if God is not the answer, what is? Pullman proposes love: when Lyra and Will become lovers near the end of *The Amber Spyglass*, the flow of Dust that has been threatening the universes eases: "The Dust pouring down from the stars had found a living home again, and those children-no-longer children, saturated with love, were the cause of it all."

This is touching, and probably satisfying to the young adults who are Pullman's target audience. Older readers—and the trilogy has deservedly drawn a great many of them—may perhaps be forgiven for wondering whether things are really so simple in this or any other universe. If love were the exclusive answer, the world might be a better place. But it is not, it never has been, and I fear it never will be. Maybe George Bernard Shaw went too far in writing, "When two people are under the influence of the most violent, most insane, most delusive and most transient of passions, they are required to swear that they will remain in that excited, abnormal and exhausting condition continuously until death do them part." Yet who with a few gray hairs, or more than a few, has not awakened at three in the morning and glumly mused along with F. Scott Fitzgerald: "It is in the thirties that we want friends. In the forties we know they won't save us any more than love did"?

Please don't misunderstand me. Occasional warts notwithstanding, His Dark Materials is an outstanding work. You don't need me to tell you that; all three books in the trilogy have received outstanding reviews and a slew—almost an embarrassment of riches—of awards. Fair enough—they deserve them. Two of the hardest things a YA writer has to do are to enter convincingly into the mind of a child and to convey complex ideas in simple, straightforward language. Philip Pullman is a master at both.

Lyra Belacqua is as perfectly depicted a girl on the edge of womanhood as any in fantastic literature. She is all prickles and spines, the better to hold the world at bay and to keep it from noting—and wounding—the tenderness inside. She is quick to anger and quick to act, and she makes mistakes and has to scramble to make sure they don't turn out too badly. She is, in short, altogether human and altogether believable. Watching her grow and hoping, heart in throat, that Pullman won't kill her off are two of the joys of the series.

Will Parry is a less dramatic person than Lyra, but makes a good partner for her. Where her weakness is impulsiveness, his is his concern for his mother and his worry about his vanished father. He is slower and more tentative than Lyra, but also more stubborn—and he needs to be.

As for complex ideas—first off, as noted, the way Pullman explains dæmons is a small masterpiece of creation. In fact, he doesn't explain them at all. He simply lets us watch the setup in action and draw our own conclusions from it. No lectures. No lumps. Lyra has a dæmon. So do the other people in her world. And seeing them do things shows what's possible, what isn't and why.

The same holds true for the alethiometer. We see what it can do, first in the hands of those who have to learn painfully what each symbol not only means but implies, and who navigate the seas of meaning with charts and tables like those through which officers aboard a British man-of-war in the early nineteenth century determined latitude and longitude. Then Lyra gets to use the device. In contrast to the learned savants who struggle to tease out hints, Lyra swallows the alethiometer whole; she might have a GPS system in her head to tell her just what the device is trying to say.

We never learn just how or why the alethiometer does what it does. But how and why don't matter. Lyra doesn't know herself, or care. All she knows is how to use the gadget and what to use it for. And that is as it should be. Not many of us understand how e-mail or the brakes on the family sedan work. We know the brakes will stop the car, and we know e-mail lets us stay in touch with a cousin in St. Paul, buy potent medications without bothering to consult doctors, get stocks guaranteed to quadruple in value in the next twenty minutes, enlarge our private parts and have the opportunity to stare at "college coeds" running around in their "dormitories" in the altogether. We all take for granted things that are part of our world, and Lyra quite properly does, too.

And there is the sheer audacity of the climax. Throughout *The Amber Spyglass*, we keep thinking, *No, he's not going to do* that. *He wouldn't dare do* that! But Pullman does, and he makes it work. Not many others could have, and few of those who could have would have. His Dark Materials is not just a work about courage: it is a work *of* courage.

Finally, attention must be paid to Pullman's writing. It has the quality of effortless ease that is more often than not the result of endless invisible labor, and it is up to any challenge. Here is a quiet scene of terror for Lyra, from chapter five of *The Golden Compass*:

> She didn't finish the sentence, because Mrs. Coulter's dæmon sprang off the sofa in a blur of golden fur and pinned Pantalaimon to the carpet before he could move. Lyra cried out in alarm, and then in fear and pain, as Pantalaimon twisted this way and that, shrieking and snarling, unable to loosen the golden monkey's grip. Only a few seconds, and the monkey had overmastered him: with one fierce black paw around his throat and his black paws gripping the polecat's lower limbs, he took one of Pantalaimon's ears in his other paw and pulled as if he intended to tear it off. Not angrily, either, but with a cold, curious force that was horrifying to see and even worse to feel.
>
> Lyra sobbed in terror.
>
> "Don't! Please! Stop hurting us!"
>
> Mrs. Coulter looked up from her flowers.
>
> "Do as I tell you, then," she said.
>
> "I promise!"

His Dark Materials isn't perfect, but perfection is for the God who dies near the end of it. Like all the best YA books, it leaves both young adults and their elders with plenty to enjoy...and with even more to think about.

Harry Turtledove is an escaped historian who writes alternate history, science fiction, fantasy and historical fiction. One of the—many—reasons he flunked out of Caltech almost forty years ago was that he read The Lord of the Rings obsessively instead of doing his calculus homework. He hasn't quite done the same with His Dark Materials, but he's come much too close.

SEAN MCMULLEN

The Field Naturalist's Guide to Dæmons

Congratulations; if you are in this room you have passed your assessment examinations and been accepted as Trans-Reality Field Naturalist Cadets. In the weeks ahead you will not merely be sent into other worlds, but into other realities of this world. These worlds, also known as alternate universes, have been the subject of intense study over recent decades. They are a source of invaluable technologies, ideas, lifestyles and even historical precedents, and we may have them for no more than the cost of training cadets like you and sending them to assist the observers already in our covert "embassies." At first you will not stay for more than hours, or at best days, because you must prove yourself able to play roles and live lifestyles quite alien to ours. On the other hand, you have been recruited for your skill in role playing games, so you should have no problems. Remember, however, that this is real: if you die in this game, you stay dead. You have been assigned to Pullman's universe because you were the best of this induction of cadets. Though it is one of the more challenging trans-reality environments, the rewards of working there are correspondingly great.

Ever since the discovery of Pullman's universe, the implications of having dæmons living in symbiosis with humans has been the subject of much research in the scientific community. Any number of questions are posed by the human-dæmon symbiosis, including the possibility that humans in our universe are capable of sustaining dæmons and would be greatly enhanced by having them. You have all seen the pictures sent back from nano-cameras aboard spy probes disguised as beetles, so there is no need for a lengthy preamble here. Humans in

129

Pullman's universe have animal-shaped dæmons that reflect their true selves. Servants tend to have dogs, sailors have seagulls, warriors have wolves, lawyers have vultures, tax officials have pit-bull terriers and so on. The dæmons cannot stray more than a certain distance from their human hosts before both begin to exhibit pronounced anxiety. The dæmons of children remain plastic and change with every mood swing until around puberty. The death of either a host or a dæmon will always kill the other.

The need for a massive observation project in Pullman's universe arises from the fact that vestigial forms of dæmon symbiosis *can* be observed in the humans of our own universe. Take superheroes and super villains, by way of example. Most have a sidekick, who may or may not be expendable. Thus Batman has Robin, a companion with lesser powers who serves many of the roles of a dæmon. The superhero can speak with the sidekick during an adventure, explaining the situation for the benefit of the swarms of spy beetles whose nano-cameras are linked to blockbuster movie generators. The sidekick can also get trapped in dangerous situations more readily, generating far more interesting plots than an all-powerful, invincible superhero. Because they have similar, but limited powers to superheroes, however, sidekicks can generally keep up with them, yet still provide identity anchors for members of the audience. Some sidekicks can turn on their hosts when mistreated, however, as did the beautiful Mirage when her super villain proved willing to sacrifice her to Mr. Incredible. A dæmon would never do this.

Guardian angels and witches' familiars are another parallel that can be seen in terrestrial humans, but these are not as similar to dæmons as one might think. Guardian angels have little contact with their wards, cannot be touched and are invisible. If it comes to that, nobody is entirely sure what they do in fact do, apart from making a person feel vaguely guilty when they are about to do something naughty. Witches' familiars are closer to dæmons in job description, in that they provide help, follow instructions and tend to reflect the personality of their witch or warlock. On the other hand, familiar-dæmons of the witches of Pullman's universe tend to range great distances from their hosts, while those of terrestrial witches usually stay close.

In spite of the differences between sidekicks, familiars and dæmons, all of the foregoing points to a slight genetic predisposition to dæmon symbiosis in terrestrial humans, perhaps even flagging an inactive gene within our DNA. Can we sustain a dæmon? Should we activate the dæmon gene, should one ever be discovered? That is why you have all been trained as field naturalists and are being sent into Pullman's universe. If we ever discover that the answer to the former question is yes, we shall need to know the answer to the latter question before we decide to do something about it.

The matter of identity is always foremost in any discussion of dæmons. Dæmons are a manifestation of the identity of the host, but having your identity on display for everyone to see can have disadvantages. For example, a highly trained secret agent, a Pullman's universe James Bond, might have an eagle for a dæmon. How, then, would this James Bond look while trying to disguise himself as a waiter in a restaurant to determine whether the arch-villain at table fourteen is plotting to destroy the world, or just trying to have a quiet date? People would notice at once that the waiter who really ought to be in the company of a rather downtrodden spaniel dæmon has a magnificent eagle on his shoulder. He could always explain that he is an action hero down on his luck, but you can be sure that the couple at table fourteen would always merely discuss the wine whenever he approached them.

On the other hand, the presence of dæmons does not rule out the practice of espionage. The servant with the spaniel for a dæmon might well have dreams of greatness and adventure, and thus be a perfect recruit for an enemy spymaster. Because the servant's dæmon looks so ordinary, he would not be expected to be leading a double life. The danger is, of course, that his dæmon might become a bit neurotic because of her host's behavior, especially if her host is doing the spying against his better judgement.

Girls running away from boring domestic duties to become soldiers or sailors would have a related problem: dæmons generally have the opposite sex to their hosts, and their primary sexual characteristics would betray their hosts at once. As for the problems facing a handsome prince trying to disguise himself as a nun to rescue his true love from a convent... unless that particular order of nuns dresses their dæmons for the sake of modesty, he might as well not bother.

Changes in the host's lifestyle have been shown to be a problem with dæmons. For example, gyms on the Earth of Pullman's universe now have centrifuges on the premises, so that a man with a chicken as a dæmon can leave the bird in there with protein-supplement chickenfeed while he does a couple of hours with the weights. This way, he at least has a very strong chicken to reflect his changed body. The problem of his dæmon being a chicken remains, however. The judges of bodybuilding competitions claim not to be influenced by the dæmons of the contestants, and have even ruled that dæmons must stand behind screens so that the hosts' bodies alone are judged. This is all very well in theory, but in practice the contestant with the chicken dæmon will soon be known by reputation. In an otherwise evenly matched contest, the rival known to have a rottweiler dæmon will always win.

Dæmon behavior is something that molds the society of Pullman's Earth to a very pronounced degree. Having a dæmon is rather like attending a cocktail party at a nudist colony: one's amorous interests and intentions are on display for all to see, but then so are those of everyone else. Thus people with dæmons tend to either be quite honest in their social interactions, or a lot better at controlling urges and inclinations when their intentions need to be masked. People of all social stations are mostly very open about their identities and intentions, but those with the self-discipline and willpower to disguise the behavior of their dæmons are very dangerous and powerful.

One question concerning the "settling" of the pliant dæmons of children into the fixed forms at puberty is the very fact of puberty. Given that the sexual drive of the average teenager resembles that of a laboratory rabbit being force-fed aphrodisiacs in a pharmaceutical testing laboratory, why are all teenagers' dæmons not "fixed" as rabbits, and thus fated to remain rabbits for the rest of their mutual lives? Scientists currently have no realistic theories on this matter, and the variety of dæmon types among adults remains a mystery.

The matter of death highlights the link between dæmons and their hosts. Recent video footage from a spy beetle shows one of the sentient armored bears of Pullman's universe fighting humans and their dæmons, and it has provided a valuable insight into the life-force bond between humans and their dæmons. A wolf-dæmon slashed open by the bear bled fire instead of blood, then vanished. Her human died at once, although he had not been injured. Moments later, when another human was splattered all over the snow by the same bear, his uninjured dæmon lay down in the snow and faded away to nothing. Thus while there are advantages to having a dæmon, rather akin to having eyes in the back of one's head or a second pair of hands, one's vulnerability is also increased considerably when the dæmon comes under attack.

The origin of dæmons is another mystery under investigation, and is on the scale of puberty and death in terms of difficulty. Evidence from palaeontology is severely limited by the fact that dæmons fade away to nothing when their humans die—leaving no bones. Palaeolithic drawings on cave walls are no help either. The animals depicted with the human hunters could just as easily be the hunters' prey as their dæmons. Scientists have hypothesised that an ancient volcanic eruption could bury a human hunter and his dæmon in ash, so that excavators would find a skeleton next to a small hollow space with the dæmon's shape. So far no such evidence has been found in the Pompeii of Pullman's world, but funding committees continue to finance excavation expeditions disguised as bands of looters.

DNA analysis is a promising alternative avenue of research into the origin of dæmons. If the genetic basis for dæmons could be isolated, then its first appearance as an active gene could be traced by analysis of accumulated mutations in the mitochondrial DNA of humans from Pullman's universe—that is, the portion of DNA passed through the female line. This strengthens the possibility of humans in our universe gaining dæmons, of course. Genetic engineering could either activate dormant dæmon DNA in our cells, or could be used to splice in dæmon genes from the humans of Pullman's universe into ours. Some researchers have suggested that we did once have dæmons, but that they did not confer any evolutionary advantage, so the trait died out. Such a theory is all but untestable unless complete specimens of Palaeolithic DNA are ever found, because DNA only shows the direct bloodline of those people who survived to breed. It has even been suggested that Neanderthals had dæmons, and that they died out because dæmonless human hunters kept killing the Neanderthal-dæmons, mistaking them for game animals.

What are the actual natures of the dæmons themselves? Is a sailor's seagull dæmon a seagull in essence, or is the seagull an allegory for the nature of the host human? If transformed into a human, how would that dæmon behave? As yet we have no examples of such transformations recorded from Pullman's universe, but cases of witches' familiars transforming into humans are known from other universes. There is the rather notorious case of Greebo, the rather oversexed tomcat belonging to a witch named Nanny Ogg in Pratchett's universe, for example. This cat was transformed into a analogue-human by the magical sciences of that universe, yet although it could talk and had a fair degree of intelligence, it remained a cat. It displayed features characteristic of many human males in that it was rakish, dashing and slightly shiftless, yet the sound and video footage recorded by a spy beetle present at the transformation still suggests a talking cat in a human body. It also suggests that many human males are little more than sentient tomcats, but that is not our concern here.

Spy beetles are currently searching for just such a dæmon-human transformation in Pullman's universe, but it could be a long time before we see any results. Dæmons are a highly personal aspect of one's place in the society of Pullman's universe, and people are thus reluctant to allow them to be used in experiments. The program of medical research involving the severing of children's dæmons from their hosts at the Bolvangar research station in Pullman's universe is analogous to the experiments on human subjects in Nazi concentrations camps in our own universe in the twentieth century: most people of the respective universes find it abhorrent in the extreme. Nevertheless, such experiments could be revived in the future because of demand. Many people are dissatisfied with their dæmons, and would gladly be part of an experiment to induce change by simulating puberty—for example by injecting massive doses of hormones and eating junk food in a untidy bedroom while surrounded by piles of homework books and playing the Pullman's universe equivalent of rock music on an out-of-tune guitar. Transforming an adult's dæmon from a chicken into a lion could probably induce schizophrenia in the host, however, or even turn the host into a dangerous psychopath. Just as Nanny Ogg's cat remained a cat by nature while human-shaped, so too are the true natures of the host humans fixed. One's transformed dæmon might look and act like a lion, but it will probably retain part of the chicken-nature of the host, even if that host does not like chickens. Following the transformation, the host might well become a combination of a rather ineffective lion and a highly dangerous chicken. The effect on the human's behavior can only be guessed at, but he would probably be something of a social liability at the very best. What would happen to the dæmon should a human from Pullman's universe have a sex change operation? There are plenty of theories, but as yet no observational evidence. In short, current theory is that dæmons are manifestations of their hosts' true identity, and definitely not animals.

It has been proposed that intelligence generates dæmons, yet the existence of the sentient armored bears of Pullman's Earth presents a very definite obstacle for this theory. These bears are clearly smarter than the average bear in our universe; in fact, they have sufficient intelligence to make tools, weapons, armor and strongholds. They also have language and advanced social organisation, and even have certain skills in perception and anticipation that are superior to those of humans. They do not have dæmons, however. This suggests that Pullman's universe is not the cause of dæmons existing. Rather, they would seem to come out of the genetic heritage of humans. Certain individual armored bears have shown an interest in acquiring dæmons, however, in an attempt to incorporate certain so-called progressive aspects of human civilization into bear civilization. This has generated vigorous debate in the bear community in the form of fights to the death in which the loser's heart is ripped out and eaten in front of the spectators. The current feeling in bear circles is that dæmons are all very well for humans, but that a bear's true soul mate is a custom-built suit of armor.

It is ironic that at a time when we are seriously contemplating the introduction of dæmons in this universe, experiments are being conducted into weakening the links between people and their dæmons in Pullman's universe, or even separating people from their dæmons altogether. At the Bolvangar research station, experiments involving a dæmon-shielding mesh of manganese-titanium alloy and surgery were able to reduce people's dæmons to little more than pets or fashion accessories. The effect on both humans and dæmons was rather akin to that of a lobotomy in the humans of our universe in that the subjects became quite compliant, but lacked drive and initiative. While this is wonderful for leaders, in terms of having one's orders followed to the letter, it can mean disaster if an important decision has to be made quickly while the commanding officer is away sitting on the toilet and having a cigarette with the communications link disabled because he does not want anyone to see that he has taped over the smoke detector. The destruction of the Bolvangar research station has been attributed to this very lack of initiative.

As the title suggests, this is a field naturalist's guide to dæmons, and is intended as an introduction to major issues for those observing and studying the phenomenon of human-dæmon symbiosis in Pullman's universe. We need to gather much more data on the symbiotic relationship than is currently available because of the large number of research projects involving genetic engineering to breed terrestrial humans with dæmons. Your brief as field naturalists is to observe dæmons and their humans in their normal state, as well as the dæmons of sick or injured humans. You should also be gathering statistics on the rate of psychological disorders on the Earth of Pullman's universe, such as schizophrenia, paranoia, depression and suchlike. Advocates of the introduction of dæmons to humans within our own universe maintain that rates of mental illness in humans in Pullman's universe are much lower because of the comfort, company and tranquilizing effects of dæmons. Many funding committees have already been convinced by such ideas, in spite of a lack of statistical evidence one way or another, so part of your brief is to provide that evidence.

Some of you, presumably those with a very good health insurance scheme, have volunteered to study the armored bears. Personally I think that this is about as sensible as inventing a time machine and trying to prove that the tyrannosaurus rex was warm-blooded by means of an anal thermometer, but the value of any observational work involving bear society is beyond question. Although they have a lot in common with a dangerous psychopath with a migraine, some aspects of the armored bears' psychology resembles our own more closely than that of the humans of Pullman's world. The bears are always individuals, just as we are; they have cannot ever have companionship that can be trusted absolutely. Footage shot at one of the royal courts of bears reminds some observers very strongly of the courts of the early Middle Ages in Europe, where tribes were trying to amalgamate into civilizations like that of Byzantium—but without quite knowing how to do it. When uncertain about their place or identity, the bears followed the example of their preferred leaders, while the humans of Pullman's universe looked to their dæmons whenever they needed to confirm their identity. Once again, this suggests that dæmons might be a superb way of enhancing the best aspects of intelligence while tempering the worst. Self-doubt, depression, extreme aggression, paranoia and many forms of anxiety could become things of the past. If this is the case, we need dæmons. So do the armored bears, if it comes to that, but arguing the case to bears while avoiding being splattered over a wide area would be a very impressive feat of diplomacy.

In all your work in Pullman's universe, always remember that you are field naturalists, with a brief to study dæmons and their human hosts in their natural environment. To do this you must fit in perfectly, so as not to arouse the suspicion of the locals and provoke out-of-character behavior. Each of you has been issued with a genetically enhanced talking hamster that will be your dæmon-analogue. Its conversation will not be brilliant, but remember that it is indispensable camouflage. Telling people that your dæmon was not feeling very well this morning and decided to call in sick will not work. With no dæmon you would appear to be grossly disfigured, or some sort of pervert, or a combination of the two. Try shopping at the supermarket with an ear grafted onto your nose if you want to simulate the reaction. Be seen to be whispering to your hamster often, and try to pretend that most of its replies do not merely involve sunflower seeds and lettuce. And one last word of advice. Sew a plastic lining into one coat pocket and always keep a handful of sawdust in it. Dæmons do not have bodily functions. Hamsters do.

Sean McMullen is one of Australia's leading sf and fantasy authors and has over a dozen books and five dozen stories published or sold. He is the winner of thirteen awards for sf and fantasy, and his international sales include the USA, Britain, France, Poland, Russia, Romania, Italy and Japan. He works in scientific computing but is currently doing a Ph.D. on Medieval Fantasy Literature at Melbourne University, where he is also an instructor at the campus karate club. Before he began writing, Sean spent several years in theater and as a musician.

$$NATASHA\ GIARDINA$$

Kids in the Kitchen?

His Dark Materials on Childhood, Adulthood and Social Power

When I was a kid, I loved to cook. I even had my own cookbooks—the sort that said things like: "Put one cup of flour, a knob of butter and a small handful of sugar in a bowl, and squish the mixture with your hands until it looks like breadcrumbs. Ask your mother to slice two apples into small pieces. Remember, knives are dangerous and you could cut yourself, so always ask an adult to do this for you!"

From these cookbooks I got the impression that if I were left alone in the kitchen I would inevitably cut myself to ribbons with knives, scald myself with boiling water and probably beat myself to death with the wooden spoon. These cookbooks transmitted a range of ideological messages about childhood and adulthood. They assumed that children were automatically less capable at performing kitchen tasks than adults were, and that adults, in contrast, would perform the same tasks perfectly and without injury. More than that, they implied that the role of adults was to stand in the background of child activity to deal with all the difficult bits, while the role of children was to obey the adult rules about "dangerous stuff" and learn the skills they would need to become successful adults of the future. Perhaps it was my mother's frequent trips to hospital to get cuts stitched and burns dressed that made me wonder why the books assumed Mum would do things so much better than I could, in the face of all evidence to the contrary.

These ideas about childhood and adulthood are embedded throughout the artifacts of Western cultures: they are part of how we as adults have perceived childhood, children and our responsibilities to them.

Literature written for children contains these ideologies as well, and children's fantasy fiction, particularly over the past hundred years, has used a range of textual strategies to position children to accept these ideas. Over and over again, children's fantasy stories have contained the same message for kids: "Have fun in the kitchen/magical kingdom/land of adventure, but leave the difficult things to adults, who know best, make wise decisions and are looking after you for your own good." It's a successful ideological recipe, which forms the basis of books as wide-ranging as *The Wonderful Wizard of Oz*, *The Lion, the Witch and the Wardrobe* and *Harry Potter and the Philosopher's Stone*. Yet while the children's fantasy tradition supports the social hegemony of adults over children, Philip Pullman's His Dark Materials breaks with this tradition to validate children's skills and culture, to challenge the idea that adults are more capable than children and to argue for a more democratic power relationship between the two groups.

From a biological perspective, the relationship between adults and children seems at first to be very straightforward. The role of adults is to look after children until they are capable of looking after themselves. Of course, any adult who has ever been responsible for a child wishes that it were this simple. While biology may seem logical and straightforward, the cultural relationship between adults and children is actually highly complex and fraught with innumerable tensions.

Over the past four hundred years, adults in Western cultures have spent a great deal of energy pondering, debating, defining and redefining the idea of childhood. Adults have variously considered children as blank slates, unsullied humans, savages, angels and sinners. We have defined children according to their future roles: as apprentice soldiers, empire builders, wives and mothers. We have also sought to define childhood in a social context: as a valuable social commodity, as a period of innocence, as fragile, endangered, and besieged by social perils and predators. All of these ideas imply that children are dependent on adults: we must teach, discipline, protect, defend and nurture children so that they can remain safe in the walled garden of childhood while they prepare to become good adults. The agency and power of the relationship clearly rest with adults, while the roles we have defined for children are relatively passive: children are to learn, obey and simply be.

Significantly, we adults rarely question our right to regulate children's lives for their own good; perhaps Kipling would have defined it as the "grown-up's burden." As part of this unspoken social hegemony, we want children to accept our control over their lives, because it is, apparently, "natural." Children, however, have their own ideas, and often contest the powerless roles we allot to them. For example, the rhymes, games and lore that children practice amongst themselves often symbolically remove the adult from the agent's position and place the child there instead. Archives of children's cultural artifacts collected over the twentieth century by researchers such as Iona and Peter Opie and Alison Lurie reveal a distinctly anti-adult sentiment, like my own favorite rhyme during childhood: "Row, row, row your boat, gently down the stream. Throw your teacher overboard, listen to her scream!" Indeed, children's culture resists the power of the adult hegemony; it is a cultural space in which children create their own rules, hierarchies and values and symbolically (and sometimes practically) subvert the power of adults over their lives.

Children's literature occupies an important position in the social relations between adults and children. Written by adults for children, it has functioned as a communiqué from the powerful to the powerless, reflecting adult values and ideologies of childhood. Thus, children's literature has typically included messages like "adults know best," "parents are benevolent (or at least benign)," "childhood is all about learning necessary adult skills" and "children should look to adults to solve their problems when things get tough." As is evident in the artifacts of children's culture, kids can be quite resistant to adult values and moral lessons, but one of the ways children's literature, particularly children's fantasy literature, has circumvented this problem has been to conceal these adult values under a surface ideological layer that seems to be aligned with the subversive culture of children.

We don't have to read a great deal of twentieth-century children's fantasy fiction to find feisty young heroes, who, with the aid of magic, intelligence and a fair dollop of luck, manage to save civilization from some witch, evil overlord or other black-hat-wearer. Usually these heroic kids journey far from the safety of home and family to have their adventures, perhaps travelling through a magical wardrobe, on a train, by hurricane or with flight-inducing fairy dust.

Really cool heroes pit themselves against adult authority figures and break adult rules to fulfill their quests. The boarding-school setting can fill this niche perfectly, allowing plucky protagonists to break school rules, traverse out-of-bounds corridors, steal restricted potion ingredients and roam forbidden forests. In tune with the spirit of children's culture, these books show the child at the center of the action, a powerful agent fulfilling prophecy or destiny for a greater good, while adult authority figures like parents, teachers and government officials are left impotent and helpless on the sidelines.

It's an attractive image for kids, because it reverses the real-life power relations between adults and children; however, a deeper analysis of these same stories reveals the adult values that saturate them. The kids may believe they're in the kitchen by themselves, breaking eggs and wreaking havoc, but they're either in a kiddie-safe play kitchen with rubber knives and a light bulb oven, or there's inevitably an adult on hand to take care of things when the dangerous stuff goes down.

Children's fantasy from the earlier part of the last century generally adheres to the play kitchen model. In stories like *The Wonderful Wizard of Oz*, *Peter and Wendy* and *Adventures of the Wishing-Chair*, the child protagonists go off to a safe secondary world to have their adventures. Because they are no longer in a space controlled by parents, teachers or other authority figures, these children are free to do their own thing, to prod buttock and to take names. So Dorothy can vanquish wicked witches, while the children of Neverland triumph over the dastardly pirates and Mollie and Peter eat scrumptious things in Fairyland.

The Lion, the Witch and the Wardrobe also follows this model to some degree, and elegantly highlights the inherent problem: when the children return from their magical world, the real world remains unchanged. Indeed, the four Pevensie children grow to adulthood in Narnia, but regress to childhood when they come back through the wardrobe. Even more importantly, the positions of power these children enjoy in the magical world do not translate into a real-world setting; adults remain in control of their lives, and the kids accept this because it is right and natural. In other words, children may be head chefs of the play kitchen, but they still can't make an apple pie.

Over the course of the twentieth century there was a growth in more serious fantasy stories for children, with deep themes and cosmic battles. Unlike the play kitchen model, kids in these fantasies don't get to play in worlds that have had their sharp edges removed; instead, the kids often have to cope with quite a lot of dangerous stuff in the kitchen, like Bilbo in *The Hobbit* (who is not a child, but certainly takes the child's part in the story), Will or the Drew children in Susan Cooper's The Dark Is Rising sequence, or the very famous Harry Potter in the earlier stories of the series. These children may seem to be powerful agents, but significant adult authority figures appear at crucial points in the stories to "advise," give their approval, or even save the day.

For an example of this, we need look no further than the events at the climax of *Harry Potter and the Philosopher's Stone*. Harry manages to make his way past all the traps and puzzles guarding the Mirror of Erised, and in the final chamber he confronts Quirrell and Voldemort (who is stuck to Quirrell's head). Harry finds the Philosopher's Stone, but Quirrell attacks him, trying to gain possession of it. In the ensuing struggle, Harry loses consciousness and all seems lost. But in the next scene, Harry wakes up in the hospital wing, apparently triumphant. In fact, Harry is hailed as a hero, but it was the wise, powerful and incredibly benevolent Dumbledore who saved the day, arriving just in time to rescue Harry and save the stone. For all Harry seems to be the ultimate hero of children's culture, the text's message is clear: kids just aren't capable of dealing with really dangerous things, but adults are— so kids should just let them do it.

Although *His Dark Materials* and the early Harry Potter stories were published around the same time, the two series have followed divergent evolutionary paths. *Philosopher's Stone* and *Chamber of Secrets* in particular are very true to the ideological traditions of children's fantasy. *His Dark Materials* is remarkably different: it challenges the old hegemonic and hierarchical assumptions common to many of its literary ancestors, recognizing children's capabilities and questioning the social power of adults.

One of the big differences is the trilogy's acknowledgement and validation of children's culture. Many children's fantasy stories show kids playing together: play is what kids do before the adventure begins. But because these texts portray child's play as a null state, they relegate it to inconsequentiality. Other children's fantasy stories choose not to deal with play at all, especially some of the more "deep and meaningful" epic fantasies. In these texts, the child protagonist seems to be a creature isolated from his or her peers. Yet for kids, play *is* important: it's the way they establish and maintain social networks with each other, and thus practice their culture.

In *Northern Lights*, Pullman vividly demonstrates the centrality of play to children's lives. In Chapter Three, "Lyra's Oxford" is introduced firstly as a space for play; the history, politics and adult purposes at work in the city are not half as important to Lyra as the opportunities the space presents for play. At the beginning of the chapter, we see Lyra playing with her best friend Roger, and then the focus pans back to reveal the ways that power amongst Oxford's children is negotiated through play activities. The tone of this section is surprisingly respectful: the narrator recognizes that adults rarely see or understand the purpose of children's play activities, but acknowledges that children's social relations are a "rich, seething stew of alliances and enmities and feuds and treaties."

At this point, the narrative focus moves from this scene of life and vitality to one that is infinitely more sinister: the abduction of children by mysterious forces. The threat of the Gobblers has a strong resonance in today's world: child predators are real-life monsters in our towns and cities. The threat of child predators creates a climate of fear and helplessness in the communities they prey upon, and in *Northern Lights*, this real-life issue appears in a fictional setting when the Gobblers abduct the gyptian child Billy Costa. Billy's mother is a great gyptian matriarch, and powerful within her own sphere, but when her son disappears she is powerless to act, and the text shows her standing at the crowded boatyard, isolated by her grief and terror and helplessness.

Yet around her, the gyptian and Oxford children are *not* helpless: under Lyra's direction, they pool their knowledge to work out when Billy disappeared, and then go off as a great swarm to *hunt* the hunters in an activity that is serious but also playful. This is an amazingly powerful vision of children's culture as an agentive force: the children are refusing to give in to fear and accept the passive role of potential victims; instead, they are working together to act constructively and symbolically wrest the initiative from the Gobblers.

This depiction of the active children is in sharp contrast to the frustrated impotence of Ma Costa or the adult gyptians on the wharf: "Some of the women were crying loudly, and the men were standing in angry groups, with all their dæmons agitated and rising in nervous flight or snarling at shadows." This description of the gyptians' dæmons highlights their emotional state: in Lyra's universe, a dæmon is part of a person's soul made manifest in animal form, so the nervous and snarling dæmons indicate that the gyptians' fear and frustration runs soul-deep. The text's message here is not that children are more powerful than adults—after all, neither group manages to find Billy or the Gobblers that day—but rather, that children are capable of coping in situations of adversity, and that even though they may act in different ways to adults, the results of their actions are not necessarily inferior.

Of course, while His Dark Materials validates children's culture, it doesn't sugar-coat it. Children's culture also has a dark side: in establishing the boundaries between child space and the adult hegemony, children can and do turn against those who don't fit in. Archives of children's culture and studies of child behavior reveal the jeers and torments children sometimes inflict on their peers. Put simply, kids can be very cruel and sometimes the same social relations that can create communities of children can also create destructive mobs or gangs, particularly when hate and fear are the driving emotions. Naturally, this is not unique to childhood, but part of our human nature: the physical and psychological persecution of individuals and cultures by other cultural groups is a distressing but very real feature of our recorded history.

The negative aspects of child social relations emerge in *The Subtle Knife*, as the children of Cittàgazze firstly attempt to kill a cat, and later turn on Will and Lyra. In the first incident, the image of twenty kids screaming in fear and hatred as they bludgeon a small cat with sticks and stones is particularly gruesome and horrifying, perhaps because it challenges our cherished belief in the innate sweetness of children. But because of this, it serves an ideological purpose: it demonstrates that children are three-dimensional people, not two-dimensional, romantic ingénues.

His Dark Materials validates children's social relations and shows that children acting together, whether in play or in adversity, can be so much more than the passive vessels the adult hegemony often positions them as. The second part of the text's empowering message moves from children's collective agency to the agency of the individual child. Lyra and Will have significant agency throughout the series, but what sets His Dark Materials apart from the children's fantasy tradition is the way that these characters direct events and negotiate the shifting currents of power that surround them.

Will and Lyra are not adventuring in a kiddie-safe, magical play land, but nor does the success of their adventures hinge on timely adult intervention. Lyra and Will evade and challenge adult attempts to keep them passive, and end up not only controlling their own destinies, but influencing the destinies of all the interlinked universes including Heaven and the world of the dead. Their desire to control their own lives is evident from the moment we meet them in *Northern Lights* and *The Subtle Knife* respectively: Lyra is busy finding out forbidden knowledge in the Retiring Room at Jordan, while Will is taking steps to protect his mother from nefarious characters.

In *Northern Lights*, Lyra accomplishes some truly amazing feats of daring, bravery and leadership. She swears to rescue her friend Roger from the Gobblers and she achieves this, even though she must journey far into the arctic wastes to do so; she destroys Bolvangar and leads the captive children to safety; she outthinks Iofur Rakinson, king of the bears, and helps Iorek Byrnison regain his throne; and in the end of the story, she walks bravely into the new world in the sky to discover the nature of Dust. Will's achievements are less spectacular, but just as significant: he cares for his ailing mother, he becomes the bearer of the subtle knife and he uses that knife to save and to kill.

At various stages in their journey, Lyra and Will need to interact with adults, and the way the text constructs these interactions provides further evidence of its ideological position. Leaving aside the issue of Lyra's parents, which I will discuss shortly, the children's relations with adults often exhibit degrees of co-operation and interdependence. For example, in *Northern Lights*, Lyra needs the gyptians to help her get to Roger, but the gyptians need Lyra's skill with the alethiometer to improve the odds of success on their journey north. She needs Iorek's strength and ferocity to help her reach the severed boy Tony Makarios and later her friend Roger, but it is only because of Lyra that Iorek has won back his dignity and his kingship.

At times, there do seem to be some more traditional, hierarchical elements in Lyra's relationship with certain adults, like the gyptians. Lord Faa and Farder Coram tend toward being wise patriarchs, and Ma Costa makes a very traditional Earth-mother. Importantly, though, these ties are transitory and the text reveals the gyptians to have little control over Lyra's quest: she quickly moves beyond them as she continues on her journey. In contrast, Will's relationships with adults are never hierarchical: Will refuses to be treated as a passive child, and, as in his initial meeting with Iorek Byrnison, he is quick to establish his agency. By the time the children meet the formidable Gallivespians, they are sure of their own power and will not accept being told what to do by arrogant grown-ups, full-size or not. Importantly, once the children and the Gallivespians start interacting on an equal footing, they begin to understand and eventually respect each other.

Above all else, the one thing that makes His Dark Materials so ideologically different from the children's fantasy tradition is its treatment of Lyra's parents. In the tradition of children's fantasy fiction, parents are benevolent, or at least benign. Often, of course, parents are absent from the story completely, but in these cases, there's usually a benevolent parental substitute, like Tolkien's Gandalf, Cooper's Merriman Lyon or Rowling's Dumbledore.

However, Lyra's parents are simply unique: nothing like them exists in the history of children's fantasy literature. They are neither benevolent nor benign. They are integral to the story and have an active role throughout. They are powerful, ambitious characters who twist events to their own advantage. And they are very, *very* bad. What makes them so unique is their complexity: they are not stereotypical evil overlords who control obligatory armies of darkness; instead, they are evil in very human ways. Lyra's mother controls an organization that abducts small children and slices their souls apart to make them "better." Not content to watch the action from the sidelines, Mrs. Coulter takes an active hand: she abducts many children herself, and, with "ghoulish" keenness, likes to watch them being "pulled apart." In *The Amber Spyglass*, we learn that she has abducted her own daughter and is prepared to keep her drugged into unconsciousness for perhaps her entire adolescence, in order to prevent her being tempted as Eve was. Lyra's father, Lord Asriel, may seem to be on the side of right as he rejects the control of the Authority and builds a Republic of Heaven, but he quite willingly sets about slaughtering a small child to make this glorious future happen. Both of Lyra's parents apparently believe they are acting for a greater good, as if the end justifies the means, but the fact that neither of them wants to do such things to Lyra proves that they know their actions are morally wrong, yet they do them anyway.

Lyra's parents are not just evil: they are also flawed. They are so concerned with their own careers and ambitions that they have completely abrogated their parental responsibilities: Lyra has been raised by strangers, and until halfway through *Northern Lights*, she does not even know her parents' true identities. Occasionally during her childhood, Lord Asriel would see her and give her money, but there is no sense of parental care in this relationship. The pair's questionable parenting practices are an extreme example of real-life issues affecting families today. One of the concerns of the modern age is that parents don't spend enough time with their children, that they substitute money and gifts for quality time, and that kids grow up without really knowing their parents, and without their parents really knowing them. Even good parents make bad parenting mistakes; His Dark Materials simply throws this point into greater relief than we find comfortable to deal with.

The construction of Lord Asriel and Mrs. Coulter subverts the ideology of the benevolent parent common to the children's fantasy tradition and at the same time embodies His Dark Materials' key arguments: that adults are not perfect, that there is no reason to believe that they will always act more correctly or make better choices than children will, and that therefore the adult social hegemony can be a dangerously unfair structure. Lyra herself quickly comes to realize that adults, including her parents, can sometimes make very bad decisions. In the end of *Northern Lights*, she holds Roger's dead body in the snow, and with her dæmon

Pantalaimon, acknowledges the ideologies of the adult hegemony and consciously rejects them:

> "We've heard them talk about Dust, and they're so afraid of it, and you know what? We believed them, even though we could see that what they were doing was wicked and evil and wrong... We thought Dust must be bad too, because they were grown-up and they said so. But what if it isn't?"

Because Lyra's parents are very human, Pullman allows them to learn and grow from their mistakes. At the end of *The Amber Spyglass*, there is a type of redemption for these two characters: they sacrifice themselves to destroy the Kingdom of Heaven's regent, Metatron, and to give Lyra time to find her dæmon, to live and to grow up. Significantly, though, there is no reconciliation scene between Lyra and her parents and from an ideological perspective, this makes sense. Lyra has been the agent of her own destiny in spite of her parents for so long that reconciliation here might imply a return to a parental fold that actually never existed.

While the biological imperative of the adult-child relationship still stands, His Dark Materials may signal a new evolutionary phase in our understanding of what it means to be a child and in the relationship between adults and children. The messages it sends to kids are positive and empowering: it argues that children are not inferior to adults; it recognizes that children's social relations may be maintained through play activities, but that this does not diminish their importance and it demonstrates that children's achievements can be just as spectacular as anything adults can do. At the same time, this line of argument can be very confronting for adults: it forces us to recognize our own imperfections, and it asks us to examine the ways that we have taken our power over kids for granted.

His Dark Materials provides an alternative model for adult-child relations, based on the way that Lyra and Will interact with the adults they meet on their journey. This model democratizes the power between adults and children, showing that adults and children are human, and thus equally flawed. Both have the ability to make mistakes and to solve them; therefore, they need each other, and the basis of their relationship should be mutual respect. To be sure, it's a challenge for adults to loosen the reins, to trust kids enough to let them do their own thing in the kitchen. But as Pullman's series shows, it's not about either group being in charge—it's about being together.

Natasha Giardina graduated with first class honors in literature in 2000 and is completing her Ph.D. in twentieth-century children's fantasy fiction at James Cook University in Australia. In 2001, she won the James Cook University Gluyas Prize for most outstanding postgraduate in English Literature. She currently lectures and tutors in children's literature and young adult fiction at the Queensland University of Technology and has presented papers at international conferences on ideological transmission in children's fantasy fiction.

Sources

Ariès, Philippe, *Centuries of Childhood*. 1960, 1962. Trans. Robert Baldick (London: Jonathan Cape, 1973).

Barrie, J. M., *Peter Pan*. 1911. (Leicester: Brockhampton Press, 1971).

Baum, L. Frank, *The Wonderful Wizard of Oz: The Authorized 100th Anniversary Edition*. 1901 (New York: ibooks, 2001).

Blyton, Enid, *The Adventures of the Wishing-Chair*. The Magical Adventures of the Wishing-Chair. 1937 (London: Mammoth, 1993).

Cooper, Susan, *Over Sea, Under Stone*. The Dark Is Rising Sequence. 1965 (London: Puffin, 1984).

Lewis, C. S., *The Lion, the Witch and the Wardrobe*. 1950 (London: Lions, 1980).

Lurie, Alison, *Don't Tell the Grown-Ups: Subversive Children's Literature* (London: Bloomsbury, 1990).

Opie, Iona, and Peter Opie, *The Lore and Language of Schoolchildren* (London: Oxford University Press, 1959).

Pullman, Philip, *The Subtle Knife* (London: Scholastic, 1997).

———, *Northern Lights*. 1995. 2nd ed (London: Scholastic, 1998).

———, *The Amber Spyglass*. 2nd ed (London: Scholastic, 2001).

Rowling, J. K., *Harry Potter and the Philosopher's Stone* (London: Bloomsbury, 1997).

———, *Harry Potter and the Chamber of Secrets* (London: Bloomsbury, 1998).

Thompson, Michael, Catherine O'Neill Grace, and Lawrence J. Cohen, *Best Friends, Worst Enemies: Understanding the Social Lives of Children* (London: Michael Joseph, 2002).

Tolkien, J. R. R., *The Hobbit*. 1937. 4th ed (London: Allen & Unwin, 1981).

DAVE HODGSON

A New Eve

Evolution of Sustainability across Many Worlds

Alongside the adventures, the love story, the battles and the fantasy, His Dark Materials holds a crucial prophecy: Lyra is to become the new Eve. This Eve's purpose is not made fully clear, except that she should restore the Dust and begin to build a "Republic of Heaven." But how will the members of this new republic behave? Like the previous regent of heaven who kept his predecessor alive in a box and those who endeavoured to destroy Dust, calling it "sin"? Clearly not. In fiction it's easy to delineate between good and evil. At the end of *The Amber Spyglass* we're left with the confidence that if Lyra succeeds she will begin a new direction for *Homo sapiens*: a new lifestyle that better values biodiversity, that harvests resources more sustainably and that acts unselfishly for the benefit of others.

With these optimistic thoughts we can all retire to our normal lives, do what we can to help the planet, sponsor an elephant calf, recycle milk cartons or help old ladies cross the road. But to settle down and wait for a sustainable future to evolve ignores some quite depressing scientific issues. Despite our best intentions we are, by evolutionary design, very selfish creatures. The logic of natural selection, the mechanism for evolutionary change that dominates modern biological thinking, shatters any illusion that we may easily transform ourselves into selfless creatures. Natural selection pays no heed to long-term stability, to caring and sharing, to selfless acts of altruism, to the "rights" of other organisms to exist. Instead, evolution is all "Me! Me! Me!," and often even more selfish than that. No matter how "nice" and "careful" Lyra is, a new republic based on altruism and prudence will FAIL.

Or will it?

But first, a short refresher on natural selection and evolution. Evolution is simply change through time, the observation that living things have changed and evolved over time. Natural selection provides the mechanism of that change. Evolution through natural selection emerges from consideration of two basic facts of nature:

> First, all organisms tend to produce far more offspring than will make it to adulthood. And of those that do make it adulthood, not all will successfully find a mate and reproduce.
>
> Second, there is a significant amount of variation within any species, much of which is genetically based and passed on from generation to generation. This variation plays a large role in determining which organisms survive and which do not.

Combine these ideas and the result is the theory of natural selection. The organisms that breed are the winners; their genetic makeup was better suited to survival and reproduction than those that failed to breed. Therefore the average genetic makeup in the next generation is different from that in the previous generation. The next generation is, infinitesimally, better suited to survive. Over thousands of years, these changes accumulate until the organisms, or some sub-group of the organisms, have changed dramatically, sometimes becoming an entirely new species. This is what is meant by evolution by natural selection.

So not all evolution is evolution by natural selection. The transformation from egg to larva to pupa to moth is not considered biological evolution, but the development of this life cycle from a simpler egg-nymph-adult cycle, over many generations of mutation and selection, is. Biological evolution should also be distinguished from cultural evolution, which is the learning of new skills from others, with no direct change in genetic material.

So we have two building blocks of biological evolution: variation and inheritance. Natural selection, Darwin's famous evolutionary mechanism, takes place when individuals compete for limited resources; the best resource-gatherer wins and the winner passes genes for skillful resource-gathering on to its offspring. It is a game of numerical domination: better genes spread through a population, only to be replaced later by even better ones. These pejorative terms, better and best, are made scientific by defining "fitness" as the ability to, or speed of, spread through a population. Genes can be fit or unfit, but so can genotypes, the combinations of genes that make individuals.

Evolution by natural selection works at the level of the individual, and cares nothing for the group. Physical features, lifestyles, behavior and interactions with others do *not* evolve "for the good of the species." The idea of species-level selection, perhaps the commonest scientific misinterpretation since Copernicus showed us where we actually are, is often called "BBC Evolution" in the UK, thanks to its promotion by narrators of natural history television. Parasites do *not* evolve to be less virulent "to keep their hosts alive" (they evolve to be less virulent in order to increase their chances of reproduction and survival). Prudence is *not* the best way to harvest resources (the prudent individual will be out-competed by the imprudent). Natural selection does *not* favor diversity. Instead, natural selection promotes exploitation, competition and cheating. This is the scientific position that really titillates evolutionary biologists because of the questions it raises. If selfishness and imprudence evolves, then why are we still here? How long until we go extinct? If everything is in a vast, never-ending competition, then why are so many different "things" still around? And *why*, if I should be looking out for number one, am I urged to help old people cross the road, risking life and limb when I don't even want to be on the other side? I thought only the fittest survived? Questions like these represent the major paradoxes of modern evolutionary biology: the evolution of altruism (why are we nice to each other?), the evolution of prudence (can we exploit resources sustainably?) and the maintenance of diversity (how do species and/or genotypes coexist?). It's only having learned that altruism, prudence and diversity are all very unlikely that the evolutionary biologist can try to find exceptions to the rule: are there any situations in which sustainable living is evolutionarily sustainable? Fans of his books will be pleased to hear that Pullman, whether accidentally or by design, provides a set of conditions in which altruism and prudence might, just might, be favored by natural selection. So there *is* hope for Lyra's Republic of Heaven. Maybe. But first we have to be clear about why a society of altruists is so unlikely.

Imagine a tribe in which everyone instinctively cooperated with each other. We'll call this tribe, and its individual members, Cooperators. Imagine another tribe in which everyone looked out for themselves. We'll call this tribe, and its members, Freeloaders.

The Cooperators would beat the Freeloaders eight ways from Sunday. They'd be better on the hunt and better at warfare. They'd out-compete the Freeloaders handily and wipe them off the face of the Earth. They wouldn't need to waste resources on fences or door locks or chastity belts. Needless to say, the Cooperators would be nothing at all like us.

But why aren't we like the Cooperators, if they are so superior? Why didn't we evolve that way? The reason we didn't is, as I said earlier, that evolution doesn't work at the group level; it works at the individual level. Imagine a Freeloader born into the Cooperator tribe. He would be a fox let into the hen house. He would cheat in every way possible, avoiding work, stealing, sleeping with his neighbor's wife, etc. The Freeloader would out-compete and outbreed his more trusting brethren. Soon Freeloaders would outnumber Cooperators, who would be slowly squeezed out of existence. This is the unfortunate logic of natural selection.

But natural selection isn't the only mechanism of biological evolution. Something different can happen when populations are fragmented. When small groups are created (maybe the Himalayas are colonized by a small group of giant bears, or a Mulefa village is bisected by a new river channel), each group may be a biased sample of the population. This bias, maybe in favor of altruism or prudence, can set a whole new course for the evolutionary pathway of the new populations. Even if there isn't a strong bias, small groups are prone to an evolutionary mechanism called genetic drift. Just by chance, genes that wouldn't be favored by natural selection might become "fixed" in a population; in other words, everyone in a future generation inherits that gene, more by chance than because it's a useful gene to have. Thus luck (good or bad) becomes an important part of the evolutionary process: populations grown from small founder groups may suffer high rates of genetic disease or may have thickened heels, just great for kicking, or may be very small. This genetic drift may set the group on entirely novel evolutionary pathways, driven by natural selection or further drift, leading perhaps to further reduction in size, the sequestering of toxins and the development of heel spurs. And flight? Just ask the Gallivespians. Note the crucial difference between the processes of natural selection and genetic drift: population fragmentation into small groups. This will become important as we try to find an evolutionary mechanism that favors prudence and altruism, a mechanism that gives us hope for Lyra's Republic of Heaven.

For now, however, consider Lyra as a new Eve. She's a good person; she cares about others; she saves people from death and even when she can't she saves their ghosts from purgatory. She hates to see resources wasted and savors biodiversity. Not only that, she's highly skilled, or at least gifted, at sustainable resource use. She managed to stem the vast flood of Dust from the world of the Mulefa, a flood that could have killed all sentient life, simply by having pure adult love. What a brave new start she could engender: her offspring would share her generosity and prudence; their offspring would inherit these traits, and their offspring, and so on, creating a new population of humans with responsibility for a vast biological empire of behavioral and ecological goodness. That was the vision that Metatron tried to destroy, the competitive lifestyle that the Consistorium wanted to squash and the fragile future whose rescue brought Lord Asriel and Lady Coulter together in mutual, fatal sacrifice.

"Fragile" turns out to be a good adjective for Lyra's Republic of Heaven. As we saw, a population of the selfless is very vulnerable to a few selfish individuals. The gene for selfishness may not exist in Lyra's new republic, but it can emerge *de novo* via mutation. And if it does, it will spread. Altruism is costly: you use resources by being nice, resources that either go directly to the other party (here, have a piece of marzipan) or get used up as part of the action of being nice (introduce yourself, take her arm, look left and right, cross the street, walk slowly, warn off cars, carry her bag, give her directions, cross back over...it's exhausting!). A cheat will simply accept resources without repayment (thanks very much! Now get lost) or watch as the altruist wastes time and effort (Ha! You wouldn't catch me helping old ladies). With more resources, the cheat will sire or give birth to more offspring, and the cheating gene will spread through the population. It's inevitable.

Cheating is as damaging to hopes of sustainable resource use as it is to altruism. In 1968, Garrett Hardin famously developed the ideas expounded in 1833 by W. F. Lloyd, and described a simple model that he called the "tragedy of the commons." Here is a Pullmanesque version of the argument. In *The Amber Spyglass*, the Mulefa seem untroubled by issues of overpopulation. Were it not for the devastating effects of the disappearance of sraf, there would be plenty of trees and seeds to go round. Groves of trees seem to be shared by communities, everyone chipping in with costs of maintenance but reaping the rewards of the seeds they collect. However, imagine if the Mulefa population grew large and, although the land remained communal, each individual "owned" trees and had exclusive rights to the seeds from their crop. Here is an economic situation similar to the grazing of common land in medieval Europe, when sheep belonged to individuals but the land was communal. In that example, it always benefited each farmer to add one more sheep to their flock. Individual gains outweighed communal losses and the land was ruined due to overgrazing. In our example, there is a large, direct benefit to the individual Mulefa of planting another tree. But too many trees exhaust soil resources; this affects the entire Mulefa community. Large, short-term, direct benefits (get more seeds for me) will always outweigh small, long-term, indirect costs (all the trees are starving) and, to paraphrase Hardin's words, "Ruin is the destination toward which all Mulefa rush. Freedom in a commons brings ruin to all."

Hardin also discussed the problem of "fouling one's own nest." Imagine if lots of people owned subtle knives. The direct benefit, to the individual, of using the knife (travelling to a new world) far outweighs the indirect cost (to everyone) of creating a new Specter. Eventually, selfishness would lead to many windows and murderous densities of Specters. Where cheats evolve, sustainability seems impossible.

Cheating is a famous trick, and has been the nail in the coffin of many a sustainable enterprise. For example, there's very little wrong with the basic definition of the socialist philosophy, everyone working for mutual benefit and common rewards—but cheats tend to ruin the party by abstaining from work or by exploiting others. Similarly in the natural world, mutualisms and symbioses can be very tenuous, fragile relationships. There's a fine line between mutualism, the coexistence of two or more species or genotypes with mutual fitness benefits, and exploitation. Take ants and aphids, for example: aphids secrete honeydew because their food supply, plant sap, is just too sugary. Ants know a good thing when they sense it, and they harvest the honeydew. In return, they protect the aphid "herd" from ferocious predators. It's all lovely and potentially sustainable, but what happens when the ants aren't getting enough protein elsewhere? Say goodbye to sweet Miss Aphid. What about if the plant runs out of sap? No amount of antsy encouragement will convince the aphids to stay; they just have to run or fly away quicker than the ants can catch them.

We can expand the Mulefa example. In their dramatically simple ecosystem, with apparently little to fear but the tualapi, they have developed what could be an obligate mutualism with a species of tree. Without the wheels provided by the tree's seedcase structure, the Mulefa's versatile lifestyle would disappear and they would have to stumble around on pegs (although their young seem to do this quite happily). Without the seed dispersal provided by the Mulefa's need for speed, the trees would compete for light in dense groves and suffer fitness costs. Through evolutionary time, these mutual benefits have coevolved into some kind of mutual dependency. *But* there is always scope for cheating. Imagine a mutation in the tree genome that makes a weak seed case. Not a very good wheel, but it looks just like the others. If the Mulefa don't spot the fake, the seed will be used as a wheel but will break relatively soon. The tree still gets its seeds dispersed, but it didn't have to put all that effort into making a strong seed case. Instead, it can divert resources into making more seed, or growing taller. Cheats win. Imagine a Mulefa that doesn't look after the seed. It gets free wheels but doesn't bother wasting energy on gardening when they break. Energy and time saved is diverted into more feeding or making more offspring. Cheats win.

This is all getting a bit negative, and slightly off-track. The question is, can Lyra's Republic of Heaven be a sustainable one? Or, even more fundamentally, can a sustainable, altruistic civilization continue indefinitely? Is sustainability sustainable?

Maybe genetic drift can help. In large groups, natural selection will favor selfish, exploitative genotypes. In small groups, though, traits can dominate populations just by chance. Lyra would make a great start as long as she could isolate herself from competition with other humans. A new colony, a brand-new republic somewhere *else*, would be dominated by Lyra's altruistic, sustainable lifestyle. However, this is not a sustainably sustainable culture. As the colony grows selfish, cheating mutants will appear, gain fitness benefits and dominate the population. For genetic drift to help our quest for a sustainable future, Lyra's republic would have to go through repeated "bottlenecks," fragmentation of the population into small groups, possibly accompanied by mass mortality. Only then could drift cause altruism and sustainable resource use to dominate. But even this probably wouldn't work. Genetic drift is a random process, it doesn't deliberately choose "good" traits. Selfish and exploitative genotypes stand just as much chance of dominating these small pockets of human civilization. Imagine lots of small groups, regularly culled, some good, some bad, some indifferent, all drifting. Is that the fine republic Lyra is destined to begin?

This is the stalemate that had been reached amongst evolutionary biologists in the 1960s. Darwinian thinking, with its focus on the individual or gene-level of selection, made little room for selection for altruistic and prudent behavior. And yet such behavior exists in nature:

there remained a large group of biologists who believed that group-level selection was its mechanism.

The debate was broken in 1969, in favor of the Darwinists, when W. D. Hamilton proved that natural selection could favor altruistic behavior. It wasn't group selection, he pointed out, but *kin* selection. It all relies, just like genetic drift, on how the population is arranged in space. Models of natural selection tend to assume a big population, with everyone mating randomly with anyone else. In reality, space becomes a problem: unless I had the benefit of an intention craft I would be unlikely to raise offspring with someone living on another continent. What tends to happen is that, to save energy, individuals stay near where they were born. That means they are likely to encounter close relatives. Hamilton, recognizing that natural selection actually promoted the spread of genes, not necessarily whole genotypes, through populations, defined something called *inclusive fitness*. At one extreme, he suggested, it would be possible for an individual to completely forgo any reproductive opportunities but still have fitness. How? By helping its relatives to reproduce. We share genes with our kin, and it is sometimes possible to increase the rate of spread of those genes by helping siblings, parents and cousins to have lots of offspring. In other words, what looks like an altruistic act (using a sting to protect someone else, studying sraf to understand the sudden death of trees) is actually selfish; it exists to protect and propagate one's own genes. There was little evidence of kin selection in the Coulter family until the end of the trilogy, when mother and father sacrificed themselves (and any reproductive opportunities that lay in store for them) to ensure the survival of the new Eve. Would they have done the same if Lyra had not been their daughter?

Acts of kin-selected altruism are easiest to perform when we can recognise our relatives. For example, Mrs. Coulter and Lord Asriel knew that Lyra was carrying their genes. However, this level of awareness is not necessary for natural selection to favor altruistic acts. All that is required is a certain correlation between who you meet and where you meet them. This was the discovery of another crucial, but often overlooked, evolutionary biologist called George Price. His story has a sad ending, but let's start with his outstanding contributions. Price came up with an equation to describe how natural selection proceeds. Maybe that doesn't sound exceptional, but his equation was so elegant and full of interpretive potential that it deserves to be seen by everyone, whether they understand it or not. Here it is:

$$\overline{w}\Delta\overline{z} = \mathbf{Cov}(w_i, z_i) + \mathbf{E}(w_i, z_i)$$

The eyes of non-mathematical readers will probably be glazing over at this point, but pay attention. Price's equation tells us that evolutionary change in some feature (e.g. how altruistic we are) is determined by a) how it tends to benefit our fitness, and b) how likely it is to be passed on to our offspring. We're talking statistics now. Quite logically, a gene will spread through a population if a) it tends to be useful to an individual, and b) it tends to get passed on to offspring.

But there is more to Price's equation than meets the eye, for three reasons. First, it extends and generalizes Hamilton's ideas of kin selection and makes them work for individuals in small, fragmented populations. Altruism and prudence can evolve if you help your relatives to reproduce, thus passing on your genes vicariously. Second, it makes it possible for spite to evolve. Spite happens when one individual goes out of their way (i.e. suffers costs) in order to hurt another individual. This is possible because, in fragmented populations, you might just find yourself in a group of individuals totally unrelated to yourself: less related than you would expect by chance. Before Price's work, spite was considered an impossible evolutionary outcome, but now we know that it can happen and an example has been found. Tiny wasps whose larvae grow *inside* caterpillars will forgo reproductive opportunities simply in order to kill members of other families who are also growing up inside the same caterpillar. What a crazy world. Sadly for Price, who was a true altruist, his proof that spite could evolve in a natural system was part of his downfall. After years of personal, religious and scientific crisis, destitute after giving all his money to the homeless, Price was found dead in a squat, having cut his own throat with nail scissors.

Price's exceptional insights have left an important legacy for evolutionary biologists, and are described here because they provide hope for the concept of Lyra's Republic of Heaven. The third novel property of Price's equation is that it says group selection *can* happen. Indeed it makes that point so well that even Hamilton was converted. If you replace "individuals" in his equation with "groups" it becomes apparent that group-level behaviors can evolve. Traits, carried by individuals, that benefit the survival of the group and the formation of new groups, can spread through a population. Thirty-five years' worth of analysis of Price's equation support the fact that, if certain restrictive assumptions are met, altruism and prudence can outperform selfishness and exploitation in the quest, driven by natural selection, for numerical domination of a population. But what are these assumptions?

Assumption One. The population must be split up into groups living in discrete patches.

Assumption Two. Groups must suffer a high rate of extinction.

Assumption Three. There must be some, but not much, migration between patches.

Assumption Four. Altruism and/or prudence must significantly decrease the probability of group extinction.

Assumption Five. Altruism and/or prudence should increase the probability of colonization of a new patch.

If all five assumptions are met, then this is what could happen. Imagine lots of patches, some of them colonized by groups, others left empty. Groups made up of selfish individuals over-exploit resources and suffer tragedies of the commons. They go extinct regularly and rarely manage to colonize empty patches. Groups made up of prudent, altruistic individuals, however, sustain their patches and rarely go extinct. Instead, they send out dispersers and migrants to colonize empty patches elsewhere, including the patches left empty after the extinction of selfish groups. Within each group, natural selection will favor the spread of selfish cheats, but as long as prudence begets new, prudent groups and selfishness promotes extinction, then an altruistic, prudent civilization might just evolve!

What has this got to do with His Dark Materials? Amazingly, Pullman provides just the right set of circumstances that could allow Lyra's Republic of Heaven to be sustainably sustainable and altruistic. "Worlds" are "patches," so groups form when individuals colonize new worlds (assumption one). Extinction could be a rather common event: the residents of Cittàgazze seem well on their way to dying out completely (assumption two). Dispersal between worlds is possible but very limited, allowed only via use of the subtle knife or via enormous anbaric explosions (assumption three). Finally, altruistic behavior and sustainable resource use would clearly lengthen the life span of new colonies (assumption four). With strokes of his pen, Pullman creates nearly all the necessary conditions for the evolution and persistence of a glorious, altruistic Republic of Heaven. But the prize is snatched away when we consider assumption five: would altruistic groups be better able to colonize new worlds? Slicing dæmons away from children to form holes in the sky doesn't seem very altruistic. The subtle knife isn't just for nice people: it has been wielded by altruistic and by selfish individuals in the past. And anyway, now that the knife has been shattered, only selfish people, those willing to sacrifice others and create Specters, can disperse between worlds. Lyra's Republic of Heaven will fail.

Or will it?

There is a way to disperse between worlds. The angels use it. Will's father used it. Pullman teases us and never reveals the solution. To build the Republic of Heaven, for it to be a sustainable and altruistic civilization, to avoid the inherent selfishness of natural selection, and to satisfy the near-impossible conditions for group selection, Lyra must learn a new way to colonize worlds. A sustainably sustainable future across many worlds? With the right Eve, just maybe.

Dr. Dave Hodgson is an ecologist, working at the Centre for Ecology and Conservation on the Cornwall (UK) campus of the University of Exeter. He lives in the middle of Cornwall and enjoys views of the North and South coasts. He and Penny share their house and garden with Merlin, the magic dog, and Patch and Bridget, the depraved bunnies. When not studying the maintenance of biodiversity, he plays drums for warblefly, the kickingest trad-punk band this side of anywhere.

Sources

Gardner, A. & West, S. A. (2004). Spite Among Siblings. *Science* 305:1413–1414.

Hamilton, W. D. (1964). The Genetical Evolution of Social Behaviour I,II. *Journal of Theoretical Biology* 7:1–52.

Hardin, G. (1968). The Tragedy of the Commons. *Science* 162:1243–1248.

Price, G. R. (1970). Selection and Covariance. *Nature* 227:520–521.

Schwartz, J. (2000). Death of an Altruist. *Lingua franca* 10:51–61.

Mrs. Coulter vs. C. S. Lewis

Someone whose grammar school is named Ysgol Ardudy and who is targeted as "the most dangerous author in Britain" can't be all bad. Philip Pullman's hideous and world-threatening offense? Pullman denies Christianity, and C. S. Lewis' Christianity in particular. Move over, Salman Rushdie, there's a Christian fatwa coming. And that's just in Britain, with a regular church attendance hovering around fifteen percent and the Queen, not God, on the currency. Who knows what will happen here in the States?

My morning paper brings me news of the assassination of the husband and mother of the judge in a case that questioned a group's right to the e-mail address "World Church of God the Creator"; the group's leader is already in jail for having tried to get the judge herself killed. The stalwart parents whose pressure has effectively and often legally removed fundamental biological truths from our schools include the ones who've fought as well to remove Harry Potter books and Jane Auel's pre-Biblical romances from our libraries. And those books don't have *anything* about Christianity or God in them, just sorcerers and cavemen. What will they do about His Dark Materials when they get wind of it???

It takes a while with these things, they not being readers and all. It took years for them to cotton onto Harry and Aiya. Even the Moslems, who are fast about such things, took a few years to notice Salman Rushdie's *Satanic Verses*, it being kind of literary and all. Just wait. (Half the young college students I've mentioned know about Pullman. But no one older I know has. *The relevant grown-ups around here don't know about it yet!* I speak from experience. It was over *fifteen years* after the publication of my dialogue *Can Animals and Machines Be Persons?* before an Imam, in a radio interview, suggested a fatwa would be appropriate for me (for having one of the speakers in my dialogue suggest that Islam wasn't fair to women). Anyhow, I'd like to propose a new word, modeled after "demonize": *Pullmanize.*

As a longtime philosophy professor and not-so-successful sword and sorcery writer, there's something else that *really* made me fall in love with Philip Pullman and the His Dark Materials trilogy. It's this. Philip Pullman masterfully and explicitly expresses a *joyous* atheism and materialism in a manner unmatched since the first modern materialist, Julien La Mettrie, cheerfully wrote in *Man a Machine:*

> To be a machine, to feel, think, know how to tell good from evil like blue from yellow, in a word, to be born with intelligence and a sure instinct for morality, and yet to be only an animal, are things no more contradictory than to be an ape or a parrot and know how to find sexual pleasure.

(Naturally, the Christian Authorities of Paris and Amsterdam burned La Mettrie's books; he wrote these very lines in flight for his life.)

For centuries there has been a tacit agreement among writers not to express or even mention atheism and materialism. Backed up into his closet or in his guarded personal life, the writer may perhaps reluctantly own to these dark isms.

I didn't. In my first teaching job, pegged by a suspicious Michigan State student, I *didn't* confess disbelief but instead simpered away with some shameful nonsense about "believing in God in my own way." An only slightly less shameful placatory line I might have employed is, "Who really knows whether there is or isn't a God?" But, of course, that *isn't* what I believe. I believe that it is *preposterous* to suppose that a supernatural being created this universe of millions of galaxies *as a backdrop* to events taking place in a perfectly ordinary planet circling an average star among the millions of stars constituting this galaxy alone. Charlie Brown's friend Linus' Great Pumpkin is more probable than that. *But Justin*, someone might say, *maybe God created the illusion of this vast array of millions of stars within millions of galaxies to test your faith!* That seems even less probable than the old one about God creating the illusion of fossils (and radioactive decay, etc., etc.) to test whether we would still have faith that the earth was created 6,000 years ago, give or take a few Biblical generations.

In any case, clear public expression of atheism is a gauche no-no, like announcing that President Dubya has his fly unzipped in a crowded theater ("How *convenient*" I can hear SNL's Church Lady sneer). Those few writers who explicitly engage with the godless material world do it *stoically*. They give us a gray god-haunted world—a world in which it is our depressing moral duty to be realistic and not give way to comforting unscientific fantasies. They know that Godot won't come but nonetheless they sit around waiting for him. They know god is dead but respectfully, and endlessly, wail at his wake—or, most commonly, they shut up about it. Only previously unknown kooks like Madalyn Murray O'Hair publicly announce their atheism and sue to get "under God" removed from our Pledge of Allegiance. Not so Pullman.

Philip Pullman agrees with Bertrand Russell's *Why I Am Not a Christian* that the Christian faith, like other monotheisms, sympathetically mirrors ancient despotisms. It is a faith unworthy of free human beings, a belief that is laced with arrogant and hateful unreason as well as comforting fantasy and mumbo jumbo. But Pullman recognizes that it is not enough to confront *stories* with facts. What we need are *counter stories*. Pullman's monstrous Kingdom of Heaven, John Milton's pride and the seed Pullman grew, is rightly and *joyously* put down at the conclusion of *The Amber Spyglass,* the climax of Pullman's trilogy. Pullman tells us that we must build the Republic of Heaven here and now and for the future. Eve rightly ate the apple of knowledge, just as Lord Azriel and his democratic allies rightly overcome The Authority. We recreate, celebrate and narrate all this as rites of passage from child to adult, from serf to citizen, from ignorance to knowledge. We are Dust and Dust is consciousness—Dust intelligent enough to know we are Dust and to tell stories about this realization, joyful stories.

Or, as La Mettrie put it while fleeing for his life, "Thought is so far from being incompatible with organized matter that it seems to me to be just another of its properties, such as electricity, motor activity, impenetrability, extension, etc." Lyra Belacqua enacts what poet Dylan Thomas wrote of a dead child, who like all of us "must enter again the round Zion of a water bead and the synagogue of the ear of corn." For Lyra liberates the underworld's ghosts by teaching them to die, teaching them to let their atoms go into the creation of new life, so that indeed "after the first death there is no other" ("A Refusal to Mourn the Death, by Fire of a Child in London").

Reviewer Michael Chabon tells us that Milton gave his epic *Paradise Lost* what he thought was a Christian and earnestly *realistic and techno-*

logical landscape, "its armored angelic cavalries shattered by dæmonic engines of war." No swords, Milton's fallen angels, they use cannons! —just as Dante must have imagined a *physical* cave, which *actually* led downward to a palpable Hell.

However, Chabon adds, contemporary fantasy epics follow J. R. R. Tolkien's model, "dressing in Norse armor and Celtic shadow…a broken fairyland." Not much science or technology in Tolkien's antiqued sword and sorcery worlds! These are worlds apart and widely *discontinuous* with our world (i.e., our universe, the whole vast, presently existing shebang). In the technical jargon of modal logic, they are worlds that are not *accessible* to our world, that are not possible futures, possible presents, or possible pasts of our world (such as a world like ours except that Dubya lost the election to Kerry—or a world like ours except that the Protestant Reformation and the subsequent Enlightenment happened not to occur, as Pullman supposes happened in Lyra's world).

Thus, taking off from our past with the lift of quantum mechanics and modal logic, Pullman gives us, among countless others, Lyra's world, which is hauntingly and beguilingly continuous with ours. Indeed, Lyra's world is so continuous with ours that the more naive reader may come away thinking that there was a Pope John Calvin who moved the papacy to Geneva. And you can touch the late Victorian brass scientific instruments as well as its arctic oiled coats and wild surmises about the far North. Call it magic realism: the seamless introduction of the *not quites, possibly so and sos*, and delicious *if this happened, then it all would have gone this way and that* which enrich realism and give it timbre, complex savor and hallucinatory visuals. Indeed, even a sophisticated reader has to know Oxford well to recognize *which* of Oxford's older colleges have different names or that my own graduate college, Linacre, is missing along with the other Johnny-come-lately colleges like Nuffield and St. Catherine's. What is termed "the science area" in my *Oxford Pocket Diary* has shrunk a bit, but Pullman saves the wonderfully Victorian anthropological collections—shrunken heads, scalps, skull-piercings, fishing spears and all—of the dusty, old Pitt-Rivers Museum. And the Royal Mail's Zeppelin station and Fell Press sandwich in next to the Oxford Rail Station and the Thames. So much for truly magical realism. "The most dangerous author in Britain" didn't earn this special endorsement for *that* but for his heartfelt indictment of C. S. Lewis' fantasies, and his racism, sexism and larded-up religion.

Indeed, reviewer Michael Chabon claims that fantasies written today follow the myth-ridden Tolkien model. And he gives C. S. Lewis'

Chronicles of Narnia as a prime example of this mode. Indeed, Lewis' Chronicles begin with the wardrobe that allows his four child characters to enter the fantasy of Narnia (Open sesame! Poof!). While Pullman's wardrobe, in which Lyra decides to hide, is a perfectly ordinary Victorian wardrobe, her *decision* to hide there, her bite of the apple, also provides her realistic entry in the account of the North that Lord Azriel gives to his curious scientific audience.

To label the Narnia Chronicles "dressing in Norse armor and Celtic shadow" is mostly, but not quite, right. And therein lies a tale, or a shaggy dog story, with which I hope to entertain Pullman, who possibly already knows it, and his defenders, who well may not. The "most dangerous author in Britain" can't be that safe. Let me add a bit of the old one-two in his defense.

In the early 1930s Lewis and Tolkien formed the Inklings, a small group that met Thursday evenings at Lewis' rooms in Magdalen College and on Tuesday noon at the Eagle and Child Pub (which the Inklings called "The Bird and Babe"). The Inklings were all male, of course, and indeed believed that real male friendship was incompatible with marriage (Tolkien, the only married Inkling, was an allowable exception to this ban, apparently because he was not thought to be close to his wife). Lewis himself had promised his closest student friend "to care for" the friend's widowed mother, Mrs. Janie Moore, if the friend died, as indeed he did, in World War I. Lewis lived with her, and his own brother, from 1921 to her death in 1951. Tolkien and Lewis also conspired to require most of Oxford's English Literature majors to read the Eddas in the original Old Icelandic version of proto-English. They restricted the all-important week-long final exams to questions about the Eddas, and subsequent developments through Old and Middle English, allowing little or nothing more contemporary than Shakespeare and Milton (Norse armor and Celtic shadows, hurrah!; down with the great flowering of the English novel, hurrah!).

Although the Inklings thoroughly enjoyed reading the manuscript of *The Lord of the Rings*, Lewis' publication of *The Lion, the Witch, and the Wardrobe* coincided with the dissolution of the Inklings in 1949 and cooled the friendship between Lewis and Tolkien. Why? Because Tolkien thought the book an improperly close allegory of Christianity in which the Lion was Christ, the female Witch, Satan, the four children, Gospel testifiers, etc. It was *too realistic* for Tolkien, who like Milton, was a fervent Christian believer. In the subsequent volumes of Narnia, Lewis apparently tried to placate Tolkien by downplaying any *continuity* between his fictional Narnia and the reality of Christ and Christianity.

When Lewis had come to Oxford as an undergraduate, he took the combination of philosophy, logic, and classics then called Greats, then clearly the most challenging and ambitious course of undergraduate study, and the prime route to a permanent fellowship at an Oxford college (or a high posting in the Foreign Office). However, Lewis' exam performance was then not enough to open an academic career. So he switched to English, a less competitive course of study, one in which he could expect to shine. And shine was what he did.

As he wrote in his diary at the time:

> The atmosphere of the English school is very different from that of Greats. Women, Indians, and Americans predominate and—I can't say how—one feels a certain amateurishness in the talk and look of the people.

Indeed, by the early1950s Lewis was already off to transatlantic fame as a popularizer for a sentimental, ceremonial and intellectually vapid Christianity. He was featured regularly in radio and newspapers. He also had long presided over Oxford's Socratic Society as its champion Philosophical Christian who would cut up secular visiting speakers to entertain his appreciative, and fervently Christian, undergraduate audience. Lewis abruptly gave up this gratifying exercise, and his Christian apologetics, when young G. E. M. Anscombe happened into a Society meeting.

Miss Anscombe, who'd moved through a First on the Greats exams to a philosophy fellowship, was already on her way to international repute as an incisive philosophical logician who did not suffer fools gladly. Deeply trained in Catholic theology as well as being a brilliant mover in modern philosophy, Anscombe found Lewis' patronizing and slovenly-reasoned religiosity vexing. Relentlessly logical, she wiped the floor with him, to the embarrassment of his undergraduate following. One of them, Derek Brewer, wrote at the time "None of us at first very cheerful. Lewis was obviously deeply disturbed by his encounter with Miss Anscombe, who had disproved some of the central theory of his philosophy about Christianity." From Anscombe's 2001 obituary notes:

> She took on (and trounced) C. S. Lewis in a debate still discussed a half-century later. Everyone present (including Lewis)

recognized that the young philosophy don's penetrating critique had undone his arguments. Some writers think that it had also undone him. A. N. Wilson...asserts that "The confrontation with Elizabeth Anscombe...drove him into a form of literature for which he is today most popular: children's stories. More scrupulous writers also portray the debate as a "humiliating experience" (George Sayer), a turning point in his life that Lewis recalled "with real horror" (Derek Brewer).

Greats got Lewis in the end.

The real Oxford—the Oxford of Roger Bacon, William Harvey, Oscar Wilde, Elizabeth Anscombe, Stephen Hawking, and Philip Pullman, the home of deep science and sharp philosophy—wasn't really either Tolkien or Lewis' cup of tea; neither was in love with the twentieth century nor, more importantly, the future. Although Pullman doesn't mention it, surely Mrs. Coulter could have ventured from her Oxford to ours like Lord Boreal, appearing here in both her seductively innocent pose and her commanding take-no-prisoners mode. Thus Lewis, the author of stories that are rife with racism and misogyny, got a well-deserved feminine double whammy, ala mode Culture. And that it was Mrs. Coulter indeed is suggested by Pullman's elimination of Anscombe's undergraduate Oxford college, St. Hugh's, from the map of Lyra's Oxford! Moreover, Pullman changes his own college, Exeter, to Jordan (where Lyra, Lord Asriel, and *Mrs. Coulter* hang out!). Not so clever to think you could get away with hiding evidence like that, Pullman! And the bench in the Botanical Gardens that Will Parry and Lyra are to sit on once each year in their respective worlds, commemorating their relation— in *Lyra's Oxford* you append a postcard from Mary Malone with a photo of the bench *in this world!* Very suspicious.

Well, the reader may ask, *we know Lewis is long dead and Pullman is happily living in our Oxford, boiling up more brazen bombast against the believers in the cauldron of his lively imagination, but what happened to your La Mettrie? Did the Authorities finally nab him?*

In early February of 1748, just when the Authorities of Amsterdam were closing in on La Mettrie, he received a letter from Frederick the Great inviting him to join the Prussian Scientific Academy and the hospitality of his Sans Souci palace. Amazingly, Frederick had anticipated that La Mettrie would need help. He welcomed La Mettrie, made him familiar company and composed and published a forthright and lengthy elegy when La Mettrie died three years later. Frederick also composed music that is still performed today, wrote poetry and a treatise on politics, allowed his citizens complete freedom of speech and brilliantly defended his state when all the major states of Europe simultaneously made war on him. Too extraordinary to be just a product of his times! Indeed and suspiciously, even Pullman's description of Lord Asriel—"a tall man with powerful shoulders, a fierce dark face, and eyes that seemed to flash and glitter with savage laughter..."—fits Frederick to a tee. Surely, if Lord Boreal and Mrs. Coulter can travel to our world, so might Lord Asriel travel to our past world. Asriel knew about Dust and world travel before Boreal and Coulter did. Yes, Frederick must have been Lord Asriel.

But then who was La Mettrie? You, if you like—but, in all seriousness, I'd prefer him to be me....

Actually, I have a sneaking suspicion that La Mettrie was really Philip Pullman. Or Pullman, really La Mettrie. Whatever.

Anyhow, let me be the first American to volunteer to be Pullman's bodyguard.

Justin Leiber is a professor of philosophy at the University of Houston. His nonfiction books include Can Animals and Machines Be Persons? *(Cambridge MA: Hackett, 1986),* An Invitation to Cognitive Science *(Oxford: Blackwell, 1991) and* Paradoxes *(London: Duckworth, 1992); his fiction includes* Beyond Rejection *(New York: Ballantine, 1980) and its two sequels, and* The Sword and the Eye *and* The Sword and the Tower *(New York: Tor Books). He did a B. Phil. at the University of Oxford, coming in first of twenty-odd on a degree for which the minimum passing requirement is the equivalent of an undergraduate first in Greats. His dæmon was Shasta IV, a cougar of the University of Houston, who had a deep rumbling purr and did loop-the-loops on the ceiling of her cage when he came alone in the evening to visit with her inside her cage. He misses her dreadfully.*

Show Me, Don't Tell Me

Pullman's Imperfectly Christian Story (and How He Lost His Way)

Philip Pullman's His Dark Materials trilogy is obviously indebted to the Christian story and derives much of its form from it. But rather than trying to write a modern Christian allegory in the fashion of C. S. Lewis, Pullman attempted to write an anti-Christian allegory based on a revisionist interpretation of *Paradise Lost* in which Satan is the hero. Pullman has made no secret that he intends his story to be offensive to Christians, and in this he succeeds (after all, to offend, it is sufficient to communicate one's desire to offend). But, his scorn for the Church aside, the religion to which Pullman's novel is opposed is such a caricature of real Christianity that most Christians would join him in rejecting it. At his best, his storytelling even advances Christian themes and values.

Pullman's best is very good, and not offensive to Christians. It's when he tries to propose anti-Christian themes that he violates the rules of his craft. I am not proposing a mere tautology here, where Pullman's writing is good when it is Christian and bad when it is atheistic. I think it is obvious that religious orthodoxy itself is not a guarantee of good writing, nor is religious heterodoxy a necessary indicator of bad writing. Rather, I want to propose neutral standards for writing a great fantasy story, standards that I believe Pullman would accept, and which, if met, would be the mark of great literature. I'll then show that His Dark Materials falls short of these standards, and suggest why he fails.

Most non-believers are what we might call religiously indifferent. They can't be bothered with the effort of developing systematic answers to the big religious questions, and so they go through their lives acting as if God doesn't exist, even though if asked, they might not identify themselves as atheists.

There's no question that His Dark Materials could be entertaining to such a person. It is well-written, imaginative and can provide a refreshing escape from ordinary life. But Pullman wants to be more than an entertainer or a writer of escapist fantasy. His trilogy addresses The Big Questions directly, and he wants his ideas to be taken seriously—especially where they diverge from Christian belief. Pullman likes to quote William Blake, who "once wrote of Milton that he was 'a true poet, and of the Devil's party, without knowing it.' I am of the Devil's party, and know it." Pullman is not indifferent to Christianity. "I'm just as interested in the Creation story as the fundamentalists are," he claims. Rather, he thinks Christianity is *wrong*, and he thinks that his stories can help make that clear to people, even save them from the errors of religious belief.

Pullman's serious ambitions commit him to a stronger view of what is possible in the genre of science fiction and fantasy than most people realize. As he himself has argued on many occasions, even contemporary fantasy novels can be works of great literature and can tell us great truths, so long as at their most fundamental level they remain realistic. In this he agrees with J. R. R. Tolkien, in many respects the father of modern fantasy, and its greatest theorist.

Tolkien thought that fantasy, what he called "fairy stories," must play by certain rules to be taken seriously as literature. Many of the rules are the rules of all fiction: the motivations of the characters have to be believable, for example. No character is fully good or completely evil. Characters have to have their own integrity as characters; just as a person is more than the ideas he has, so a character is more than the sum of the author's vague stereotypes about Scots, or gays or people from the working classes.

But there are some rules that are peculiar to the genres of fantasy and science fiction. I want to emphasize three: 1) While the nature of the genre requires that there will be significant fantastic elements in any such story, those elements can only frame the narrative, not resolve it. The deus ex machina is forbidden. The author has to explain the rules of the story ahead of time—the knight can kill the dragon with the magic sword only if he first acquires the amulet of invisibility from the wizard in the cave atop the Dark Mountains—and then the rules hold him bound. When the hero (or, more accurately, when the plot) is lost and without hope, the author is not allowed just to make something up. 2) Similarly, the fantastic elements have to put limits on the characters, and not just remove them; Superman needs his kryptonite, or else his adventures are boring as well as implausible. 3) Finally, the fantasy author has to limit expository speech severely. Presumably, the reader is unfamiliar with the world he is visiting, so the author has to spend some time introducing him to its relevant features. But it is vastly better to show those features than to have a character explain them in a speech.

This last point is more of a recommendation or a guideline than a hard and fast rule, but it is grounded in the same principle as the other rules, namely, that the goal of fantasy writing is (in Pullman's dramatic formulation) "stark realism." To make a realistic scene, the characters have to act with realistic motives in circumstances that are consistent with already established rules of the fantastic world. The chief danger of any fiction, but especially fantasy writing, is that the author inadvertently introduces to the story something that rings false, is inconsistent with the story or just doesn't make sense. Since it is easier to *describe* something completely ridiculous than it is to *depict* it convincingly, the author is well-advised to prefer showing to telling as a check against the temptation just to make stuff up. It is easy for the fantasy writer to have a character simply *talk* about something that is pure baloney; it's much harder to put the baloney in a scene and have it make sense in the context of the story.

In the first pages of *The Golden Compass* Pullman artfully introduces us to dæmons without resorting to a single speech:

> Lyra and her dæmon moved through the darkening hall, taking care to keep to one side, out of sight of the kitchen...Lyra stopped beside the Master's chair and flicked the biggest glass gently with her fingernail. The sound rang clearly through the hall. "You're not taking this seriously," whispered her dæmon. "Behave yourself." Her dæmon's name was Pantalaimon, and he was currently in the form of a moth, a dark brown one so as not to show up in the darkness of the hall....

And so on, throughout the marvelous opening chapters of the book. We discover in this brief space that there are dæmons, that they belong to people, that they change shapes, that they talk and can disagree with their humans, that they have their own names and personalities, that they are usually a person's best friend. There's a lot more to learn about dæmons, and we want to learn more, but we're willing to wait—it is much more urgent to know what's going to happen to Lyra and Pan as they hide in the wardrobe in the Retiring Room.

The Golden Compass is a great novel because it is exemplary in its obedience to this and to all the rules of realistic fantasy writing I just described. Pullman tells us precisely what we need to know about dæmons and Dust and intercision and the Magisterium, and a little less than we hunger to know, mostly by showing rather than telling. Pullman establishes the rules about dæmons gradually, and sticks to them rigorously; dæmons are the opposite sex of their human, their forms represent the moods and personality of their human, they cannot travel too far away (except in the case of witches) and even accompany their humans in death; they settle into one form in adulthood, and a human without one is spiritless and terrifying. The plot of the first novel revolves around these rules, to the point that we come to feel horror at the thought of intercission, just as Lyra does.

In The Subtle Knife, on the other hand, Pullman starts to rely on speeches to move the plot. Take, for example, chapter two. After introducing us to Will and having Will meet Lyra, Pullman switches to Serafina's point of view. Serafina eavesdrops on the inquisition of a captured witch, whom she kills before she could reveal the prophecy about Lyra. So far so good—Pullman is letting us know some important information amidst an action-packed scene. But then the chapter slows down:

> They turned south, away from that troubling other-world gleam in the fog, and as they flew a question began to form more clearly in Serafina's mind. What was Lord Asriel doing? Because all the events that had overturned the world had their origin in his mysterious activities. The problem was that the usual sources of her knowledge were natural ones...For knowledge about Lord Asriel, she had to go elsewhere. In the port of Trollesund, [the witches'] consul Dr. Lanselius maintained his contact with the world of men and women, and Serafina Pekkala sped there through the fog to see what he could tell her.

This is a ham-handed transition—the topic of Lord Asriel comes out of nowhere—and it ends with an almost apologetic indication that Pullman is going to slow down the story with some talking. A page later, Dr.

Lanselius suggests she go visit Lord Asriel's manservant Thorold, "to see if he can tell you anything." (Notice the verb—he's telling, not showing.) Serafina's interview with Thorold has one purpose: to allow Pullman to inform the reader of Lord Asriel's plans to overthrow the Authority.

This is the first of many such explanation-filled scenes over the trilogy's last two books. Almost any chapter with Serafina will include a long expository speech, as will any scene that contains John Parry or which takes place in Lord Asriel's fortress. The angel Baruch is introduced, gives two expository speeches, and then dies. Mary Malone's main purpose as a character is to explain rather than do: she explains Shadows to Lyra, she explains the Mulefa to the reader, she explains Dust to the Mulefa and finally she explains why "the Christian religion is a very powerful and convincing mistake." Her tempting of Lyra consists simply in telling stories, i.e., more explaining.

Pullman's bad habit becomes particularly frustrating when it corrupts the character of Mrs. Coulter. In the early books, she is a formidable and relentless Gobbler, pursuing Lyra to the ends of the earth and beyond. After she captures Lyra at the end of *The Subtle Knife*, though, it seems that Pullman is not sure what to do with her; for much of *The Amber Spyglass*, her narrative role is little more than to give other characters a chance to explain things to the reader. So, in scene after implausible scene, she is captured, she persuades her captors to reveal something important by asking a question and batting her eyes, and then she escapes (she does something like this to Will, to Lord Asriel, to the Magisterium, to Lord Asriel again and finally to Metatron).

All these "telling" scenes sap the narrative energy. So why does such a talented writer rely on them? I want to suggest that Pullman cannot promote his alternative to Christianity in any other way. Consider, for example, his view of salvation. As established by the Authority, death sends all people, without their dæmons, to a separate land in a different world. There, harpies remind them of their sins, tormenting them until the souls forget their previous lives out of self-defense. Will and Lyra propose to cut a hole into a different world so that the souls of the dead can leave the land of the harpies behind. The dead wonder, reasonably, what would happens to them if they were to leave:

> "Tell us where we're going! Tell us what to expect! We won't go unless we know what'll happen to us!"
>
> Lyra turned to Will in despair, but he said, "Tell them the truth. Ask the alethiometer, and tell them what it says."

...She took out the golden instrument. The answer came at once. She put it away and stood up. "This is what'll happen," she said, "and it's true, perfectly true. When you go out of here, all the particles that make you up will loosen and float apart, just like your dæmons did. If you've seen people dying, you know what that looks like. But your dæmons en't just *nothing* now; they're part of everything. All the atoms that were them, they've gone into the air and the wind and the trees and the earth and all the living things. They'll never vanish. They're just part of everything. And that's exactly what'll happen to you, I swear to you, I promise on my honor. You'll drift apart, it's true, but you'll be out in the open, part of everything alive again."

No one spoke until a young woman cam forward. She had died as a martyr centuries before. She looked around and said to the other ghosts... "This child has come offering us a way out and I'm going to follow her. Even if it means oblivion, friends, I'll welcome it, because it won't be nothing. We'll be alive again in a thousand blades of grass, and a million leaves; we'll be falling in the raindrops and blowing in the fresh breeze; we'll be glittering in the dew under the stars and the moon out there in the physical world, which is our true home and always was. So I urge you: come with the child out to the sky!"

Pullman is preaching to his readers here. What's more, he is preaching obvious nonsense about the joy of being a raindrop. Atoms are not alive, let alone conscious. To say otherwise is to promote pantheism, a silly religious belief if ever there was one. Pullman has broken all the rules of literary realism at once: Lyra has acquired a confidence about scientific matters that were completely beyond her in *The Golden Compass*; the ghost of the martyr retains enough leadership ability to make an impassioned speech, though ghosts can barely remember their own names; the alethiometer has suddenly gone from a puzzling and temperamental instrument to the source of an entirely new religion, which Lyra is able to grasp "at once." The whole scene demonstrates the sort of shallow thinking and writing which give the fantasy genre a bad name.

Significantly, this radical plot development takes place through speeches. I cannot imagine how Pullman could communicate the supposed joy of ceasing to exist except through such a speech. Here's what happens when Roger leaves the world of the dead:

He took a step forward, and turned to look back at Lyra, and laughed in surprise as he found himself turning into the night, the starlight, the air…and then he was gone, leaving behind such a vivid little burst of happiness that Will was reminded of the bubbles in a glass of champagne.

Contrast that with Pullman's description a few pages earlier of what happens when Lyra falls into the abyss into which all Dust is flowing:

As she utterly failed to hold on to anything, as the stones rolled and tumbled beneath her, as she slid down toward the edge, gathering speed, the horror of it slammed into her. She was going to fall. There was nothing to stop her. It was already too late. Her body convulsed with terror….Her whole being was a vortex of roaring fear. Faster and faster she tumbled, down and down, and some ghosts couldn't bear to watch; they hid their eyes and cried aloud. Will felt electric with fear.

We don't need a long speech to make Lyra's fear plausible—falling into oblivion is intrinsically terrifying. On the other hand, it's quite hard to sympathize with Roger's "vivid little burst of happiness" upon ceasing to exist. Just before falling, Lyra thinks that falling into the abyss "would be far worse than the gray, silent world [of the dead] they were leaving," and that seems obvious enough. But is being "atomized" (as the old space movies called it) any different? Despite the testimony of the alethiometer and the passionate speech of the martyr, it's hard to believe that's the case.

This illustrates the problem with Pullman's atheism; I maintain that it's not just false, but it's literally *unbelievable*. Pullman's description of non-existence contradicts what we instinctively believe. He insists a bit too zealously that we trust in his mere words and promises that oblivion is superior to life—rather than rely on our experience, which makes us believe the reverse. His exhortations come across as forced and phony as a result. By contrast, with its promise of heaven, Christianity is consistent with this natural inclination.

In his less preachy moments, though, Pullman's instincts are more realistic, and more consistent with the Christian faith. At the end of *The Subtle Knife*, Will pauses while remembering his father:

> He longed for his father as a lost child yearns for home... It had been five years now since that Saturday morning in the supermarket when the pretend game of hiding from the enemies became desperately real, such a long time in his life, and his heart craved to hear the words, "Well done, well done, my child; no one on earth could have done better; I'm proud of you. Come and rest now...."

This image calls to mind the parable of the talents (Matthew 25:21), in which the master tells his stewards, "Well done, good and faithful servant...enter into the joy of your master." Almost by accident, Pullman has brought to mind the Christian idea of heavenly repose. Resting with one's father is intimate and attractive, and Will's longing is entirely natural. The desire to be annihilated, on the other hand, is hard to comprehend.

Pullman's story would have been better off, I think, if he had borrowed the Christian conception of the afterlife. But instead, during the climactic scene of the whole series, he proposes that the lives of Will and Lyra will be meaningful only if they evangelize people to prepare them for death and subsequent oblivion:

> "We must make enough Dust for them, Will, and keep the window open—"
>
> "... and if we do," he said shakily, "if we live our lives properly and think about them as we do, then there'll be something to tell the harpies about as well. We've got to tell the people that, Lyra."
>
> "The true stories, yes," she said, "the true stories the harpies want to hear in exchange. Yes. So if people live their whole lives and they've got nothing to tell about it when they've finished, then they'll never leave the world of the dead. We've got to tell them that, Will."

I like the idea that a good life involves doing something worth telling a story about, and that those whose lives have no part in the truth ought not to be rewarded. Those are attractive themes—and totally Christian, perfectly compatible with "The Greatest Story Ever Told." But I think any thoughtful reader has to be disappointed with such an uninspired ending to a suspense-filled tale. I know that I was. When presented with the option of choosing Christianity and its promise of eternal bliss for those who struggle for the truth or Pullman's pantheism with its promise of annihilation for those who live a moral life (and eternal torment for those who don't), I expect that most people would prefer the Christian version of the afterlife. It's the more attractive story. Pullman's failure of imagination at this key moment is inexcusable in such a talented artist, and a result of his ideological atheism.

Let us examine another case. As we have seen, Pullman puts great weight on the power of telling true stories, and he recognizes that false stories can be poisonous to the human soul. He rejects the authority of the Church because he sees it as a source of false stories, told to persuade people to accept unhappiness in the here and now for the promise of a future bliss. As he told an interviewer, he believes that "every single religion that has a monotheistic god ends up... persecuting other people and killing them because they don't accept them." It's as if he's thrown down the gauntlet, challenging the Church to demonstrate who is the better storyteller, to see whose tales are truer and more profound. Pullman thinks his story is superior to the Christian one, and perhaps on no point does he think his advantage is greater than on his account of freedom and of the danger that authority provides to truth. It is for this reason that he chooses to retell the story of the Fall, to attack the Christian story of sin and redemption, of the need for humble submission to the will of God, at its root. According to Pullman's own standards, if his story fails here, it fails entirely. So it is worthwhile to consider this point in depth.

It appears from the internal evidence of the novels that between the writing of *The Golden Compass* and *The Subtle Knife* Pullman changed his mind about which part of *Paradise Lost* he wanted to reinvent. Recall that at the end of *The Golden Compass*, Lord Asriel gives two long speeches suggesting that his goal is to destroy the source of Dust, and that Dust is tied up with the knowledge of good and evil.

> Somewhere out there is the origin of all the Dust, all the death, the sin, the misery, the destructiveness in the world. Human beings can't see anything without wanting to destroy it, Lyra. *That's* original sin. And I'm going to destroy it. Death is going to die.

This is clearly an allusion to the story of the fall of man, the topic of the later books of Milton's epic poem. But as we saw earlier, in *The Subtle*

Knife Pullman goes out of his way to tell us that Asriel wants to conquer heaven and overthrow the Authority—a clear allusion to the *opening* books of *Paradise Lost*. The reader finds out, and Asriel is supposed to know, that destroying the Authority will not affect Dust at all, that these are two different tasks. So it seems Pullman has changed his mind about Asriel's intentions. He tries to patch up this significant amendment to the plot by having Asriel explain away one of his speeches from *The Golden Compass*—at the end of *The Amber Spyglass*, Asriel admits to Mrs. Coulter that he lied to her about destroying Dust during their passionate embrace at Svalbard. But Pullman never explains away Asriel's much more powerful speech to Lyra arguing for the same thing.

So it seems that Pullman's oldest and grandest theme, before he decided to have Asriel overthrow the Authority, was to give a different reading of the Fall. On his account, what Christians regard as the "original sin" is not a loss of innocence but a step forward in man's evolution, an increase of knowledge and therefore an unambiguous positive development. That particular spin on the Christian story has a venerable past. The theme of stealing knowledge from the gods dates back to the pre-Christian myth of Prometheus. This counter-tradition usually holds that Satan was right, that knowledge of good and evil did make man like a god and that it was an act of maturity for man to throw off all limitations to his knowledge imposed by God (and analogously, by any external authority). In this version of the story, Eve is at the vanguard of the European Enlightenment, whose essence is captured by Immanuel Kant's slogan, "Dare to cast off your self-imposed childhood! Dare to *know*!"

It is interesting, though, that Pullman does not hold this view in its purest form. Giacomo Paradisi, the old knife-bearer in Torre degli Angeli, shows that some investigations can be evil:

> "The Specters are our fault, our fault alone. They came because my predecessors, alchemists, philosophers, men of learning, were making an inquiry into the deepest nature of things. They became curious about the bonds that held the smallest particles of matter together… About these bonds we were wrong. We undid them and let the Specters in."

The assumption here is that the pride of the men of learning led to their fall. There are some mysteries that should be treated with reverence, but the philosophers in Citàgazze were too ambitious, and that led to their demise. We learn at the end of *The Amber Spyglass* that the subtle knife is responsible for the Dust leaving the universe as well as for the centuries of Specter attacks. That's a lot of evil to come from the quest for knowledge.

In the part of the trilogy that takes place in our world, the Church is not the sinister enforcer of orthodoxy that it is in Lyra's world. That role is reserved for the scientific establishment, which is too rigid to see the potential in Mary Malone's research, and is shutting it down for lack of funding. Though there might be some funding available if the research has military implications, Mary does not want knowledge to be used to kill people, so she prefers to abandon it. Just as in Cittàgazze, science here is not portrayed as a force for liberation, an unquestionable good. It is good only if circumscribed by morality—just as in the Garden of Eden.

In our post-Hiroshima world, common sense tells us that we need to discipline our curiosity by morality, that knowledge can be used for evil as well as good. This costly lesson aligns with Christianity against the naïve Enlightenment slogan of Kant. And as we have seen, Pullman appeals to this conventional wisdom in several places. Yet Pullman wants to interpret the Fall in an anti-Christian way, as man discarding moral authority and boldly asserting his right to know. Is this just inconsistent?

I think Pullman might be making a deeper point. Recall the scene in *The Subtle Knife* when Lyra first meets Mary Malone and chastises her for ducking questions of good and evil out of a respect for science:

> "D'you know how embarrassing it is to mention good and evil in a scientific laboratory? Have you any idea? One of the reasons I became a scientist was not to have to think about that kind of thing."
>
> "You *got* to think about it," Lyra said severely. "You can't investigate Shadows, Dust, whatever it is, without thinking about that kind of thing, good and evil and such."

This is a very revealing scene, because for the first time Pullman is complicating his view of religion. Heretofore, religion has been strictly a source of malevolent control over the thought of man. But now Lyra is pointing out that religion also raises essential questions about good and evil. Pullman's suggestion is that while freedom from religious authority might be desirable, that doesn't legitimize indifference to the big moral questions. Truth, liberty and goodness are all important values, and there should be a way to preserve the first two without compromising the third.

Of course, the question arises about what to do when people abuse their liberty. Can we punish them without restricting their liberty? Can we act to prevent harm to others? What if somebody wants to harm a few people, or even just one person, for the sake of some greater good, perhaps for some scientific discovery or for the liberation of mankind from tyranny—should some authority stop this? Lord Asriel's murder of Roger enables him to mount his attack on the Authority, and ultimately to free all human beings from tyranny. Do the ends justify the means? Should we have been cheering for Mrs. Coulter and the Magisterium to stop him? These are hard questions, yet Pullman doesn't really face them. He allows the Church and the Authority to be so cartoonishly evil that he never addresses the question of what a good authority might look like.

In this, too, he should have stayed closer to the Christian line, which claims that God is a king and a father, that he is merciful and patient and just, is good and kind and powerful and loving, possessing all the qualities that are desirable in a ruler. The story of the Fall is the story of angels and men rejecting such a ruler, because they thought they could live without any authority. As subsequent experience reveals that men need to be governed, and that human governors are far from perfect, it becomes clear that it was a mistake to reject the authority of the only good and just ruler in the universe. As man recognizes that liberty without morality is evil, it becomes possible to see that the only real liberty is that which is subject to goodness. According the story of the Fall, Adam rejected just this morally circumscribed liberty when he rejected God's authority. That's why it was a *fall*. Pullman acknowledges that there needs to be some government in the cosmos (the Republic of Heaven), but he gives us no reason to think that it will be good government, let alone that it will be better than the perfect providence that believers attribute to God.

Pullman's narrative slows down and rings false when he tries to lay out his anti-religious vision. When the story is really moving he often appeals to Christian views, and rather effectively at that. I think that the climax of *The Amber Spyglass* makes both points quite nicely.

There are seven chapters—about twenty percent of the novel—after the battle scene in which Lord Asriel's forces overthrow the Authority and Metatron. I found this fact surprising, because I couldn't remember that much happening after the battle. If someone had asked me, I would have assumed there were at most two chapters after the battle, one in which Mary Malone "tempts" Will and Lyra, leading to their kiss, and the second in which they discover the secret of Dust, say goodbye and return to their respective worlds. Instead, Pullman takes four chapters to get to the kiss, three of which he spends having the ghost remind Mary to "tell stories" and having Mary give witness about why she left Christianity.

And what banal testimony! Mary Malone leaves her religious order because she feels more strongly the call of her body, and decided that religious asceticism was unnatural: "for the first time ever I felt that I was doing something with all of my nature and not only a part of it." This seems an unnecessarily philosophical description for what amounts to a brief fling, but Pullman seems to think that by celebrating the goodness of bodies, he's really got the goods on Christianity and its "self-righteous abstinence" (in Mrs. Coulter's words). This story plants in Lyra's mind the idea of kissing Will—which because of the Church's hatred of the body is supposed to be the reenactment of Original Sin—and for some inexplicable reason their kiss reverses the flow of Dust.

But then something very interesting, narratively interesting, happens: Lyra and Will are forced to separate from each other forever. Pullman has laid the groundwork for this skillfully. First, John Parry's ghost tells Will and Lyra that he died because he had been separated from his world for too long, and "your dæmon can only live its full life in the world it was born in." Second, the angel Xaphania (we assume) tells Pantalaimon and Will's dæmon Kirjava that every cut with the subtle knife creates a Specter and allows Dust to escape. Together, like a neat syllogism, these facts force Will and Lyra to conclude that they must give up their new-found love in order to save the souls and dæmons of others.

It is ironic that Mary Malone's story leads to this conclusion. Mary left her religious order to find self-fulfillment, recovering from years of self-renunciation in the name of spiritual goods by attending to the desires of body. Will and Lyra, on the other hand, find themselves reasoning in a fashion not unlike that of a young person considering a vocation to religious celibacy: "Although love and marriage are great goods, I am clearly called to a greater good. It will not be easy, and I am tempted not to obey, but I recognize that my difficult life will have its own rewards, not least the satisfaction of knowing that my choice will help many other people enjoy life now and go to heaven."

Earlier, as we have seen, Pullman expresses nothing but contempt for religious asceticism, which renounces bodily pleasure for the sake of a supposedly higher love. But this dramatic ending appeals to something much like it—because it makes for a better story, as Pullman himself admits:

> The reason they have to part in the end is a curious one and it's hard to explain except in terms of the compulsion of the story. I knew from the very beginning that it would have to end in that sort of renunciation. (I don't know how I know these things, but I knew)... I tried all sorts of ways to prevent it, but the story made me do it. That was what had to happen. If I'd denied it, the story wouldn't have had a tenth of its power.

Pullman is too instinctive a storyteller to end his trilogy the easy way, with "happily ever after." In an interview, Pullman explains that Lyra and Will could not have chosen mere self-fulfillment, because that would have been to choose immaturity.

> "Live fast, die young" is exactly what responsibility and wisdom set their faces against. These two children are setting out on a far more difficult and more valuable journey, which is the journey toward wisdom. This is a story about growing up.

Being a grown-up requires struggle, self-discipline and a certain admixture of heartache and melancholy. It is not all adventure and excitement, and few things come easily. And it requires that one cease to be self-absorbed, and to care about others and the common good. This lesson is narratively and dramatically compelling, precisely where Mary Malone's account of her loss of faith is not. It's no coincidence, I'd argue, that whereas Mary's autobiography is the vehicle for Pullman's own ideas about religion, this lesson—that wisdom requires personal sacrifice—resonates with the deepest parts of the Christian story.

The Amber Spyglass, and thus the trilogy as a whole, is marred by Pullman's sanctimonious atheism. It is still an enjoyable novel, and series, but for those enthralled by The Golden Compass and led on by The Subtle Knife, the conclusion to the series can only be a disappointment. As the novel continues, Pullman succumbs to the very vice he excoriates so convincingly throughout the series—that of hypocrisy, of preaching what one does not (and if one is honest, cannot) believe. To do so he violates the very rules of fantasy writing that vaulted him to the forefront of the genre. Pullman's trilogy relies on Christian themes, but it tries to resist their power, and his resulting imperfect appropriation of the Christian story is the cause of its imperfections as a fantasy story. Were Pullman to have borrowed even more heavily from Christian cosmology and morality, his series would have been better, because it would have been deeper, more psychologically plausible, and more consistent with our experiences and desires.

Pullman has allowed Milton's Satan to tempt him. In his pride, he challenges God's story and twists it for his own purposes, but his retelling, his creation if you will, is a mere shadow of the real thing.

Daniel P. Moloney, a former editor at the journal First Things, *is a lecturer in the Politics Department at Princeton. He has a B.A. in Religious Studies from Yale and a Doctorate in Philosophy from Notre Dame. He has written for* First Things, Wall Street Journal, National Review, Crisis *and* American Prospect, *among other publications.*